Phishing Dark Waters

Phishing Dark Waters

The Offensive and Defensive Sides of
Malicious E-mails

Christopher Hadnagy
Michele Fincher

WILEY

Phishing Dark Waters: The Offensive and Defensive Sides of Malicious E-mails

Published by
John Wiley & Sons, Inc.
10475 Crosspoint Boulevard
Indianapolis, IN 46256
www.wiley.com

ISBN: 978-1-118-95847-6
ISBN: 978-1-118-95849-0 (ebk)
ISBN: 978-1-118-95848-3 (ebk)

Manufactured in the United States of America

10 9 8 7 6 5 4 3 2 1

I dedicate this book to a few people who made it possible. My amazing wife, Areesa, you are one of the most patient, kind, and wise people I have ever met. I hold on to the dream of an eternal future.

Michele, thankfully Ping made that referral a few years ago. Without you this is not possible.

Dave, as I write these words, I can't believe how far we have come. Thank you for your support.

—Christopher Hadnagy

This is for my husband, the most beautiful soul in the universe and ruler of all my domains.

And to Chris; thank you for giving me a job and believing in me.

—Michele Fincher

About the Authors

Christopher Hadnagy is the founder and CEO of Social-Engineer, Inc. Chris possesses more than 16 years' experience as a practitioner and researcher in the security field. His efforts in training, education, and awareness have helped to expose social engineering as the top threat to the security of organizations today.

Chris established the world's first social-engineering framework at www.social-engineer.org, providing an invaluable repository of information for security professionals and enthusiasts. That site grew into a dynamic web resource, including a podcast and newsletter, which have become staples in the security industry and are referenced by large organizations around the world. Chris also created the first hands-on social-engineering training course and certification, *Advanced Practical Social Engineering,* which is attended by law enforcement, military, and private sector professionals.

A sought-after writer and speaker, Chris has spoken and trained at events such as RSA, Black Hat, and various presentations for corporate and government clients. Chris is also the best-selling author of two books: *Social Engineering: The Art of Human Hacking* (Wiley, 2010) and *Unmasking the Social Engineer: The Human Element of Security* (Wiley, 2014).

Chris specializes in understanding how malicious attackers exploit human communication and trust to obtain access to information and resources through manipulation and deceit. His goal is to secure companies by educating them on the methods used by attackers, identifying vulnerabilities, and mitigating issues through appropriate levels of awareness and security.

Chris is a certified Expert Level graduate of Dr. Paul Ekman's Micro Expressions courses, having made the study of nonverbal behaviors one of his specialties. In addition, he holds certifications as an Offensive Security Certified Professional (OSCP) and an Offensive Security Wireless Professional (OSWP).

Michele Fincher is the Chief Influencing Agent of Social-Engineer, Inc. She has more than 20 years' experience as a behavioral scientist, researcher, and information security professional. Michele's diverse background has helped solidify Social-Engineer, Inc.'s place as the premier social-engineering consulting firm.

As a U.S. Air Force officer, Michele's assignments included the USAF Academy, where she was a National Board Certified Counselor and Assistant Professor in the Department of Behavioral Sciences and Leadership. Upon separating from the Air Force, Michele went on to hold positions with a research and software development firm in support of the U.S. Air Force Research Laboratory, as well as with an information security firm, where she conducted National Security Agency appraisals and Certification and Accreditation for federal government information systems.

At Social-Engineer, Inc., Michele is a senior penetration tester with professional expertise in all facets of social-engineering vectors, assessments, and research. A remarkable writer, she is also the talent behind many of the written products of Social-Engineer, Inc., including numerous reports and assessments, blog posts, and the *Social-Engineer Newsletter.*

Michele is an often-requested trainer and speaker on various technical and behavioral subjects for law enforcement, the intelligence community, and the private sector in venues including the Black Hat Briefings, RSA, Techno Security, and the *Advanced Practical Social Engineering* training course.

Michele has her Bachelor of Science in Human Factors Engineering from the U.S. Air Force Academy and her Master of Science in Counseling from Auburn University. She is a Certified Information Systems Security Professional (CISSP).

About the Technical Editor

David Kennedy is founder of Trusted Sec and Binary Defense Systems. Both organizations focus on the betterment of the security industry from an offense and a defense perspective. David was the former Chief Security Officer (CSO) for a Fortune 1000 company where he ran the entire information security program. David is a co-author of the book *Metasploit: The Penetration Testers Guide* (No Starch Press, 2011) and the creator of the Social-Engineer Toolkit (SET) and Artillery. David has been interviewed by several news organizations including CNN, Fox News, MSNBC, CNBC, Katie Couric, and BBC World News.

David is the co-host of the Social-Engineer Podcast and has appeared on a number of additional podcasts. David has testified in front of Congress on two occasions regarding the security around government websites. David is one of the co-authors of the Penetration Testing Execution Standard (PTES), a framework designed to fix the penetration testing industry. David is the co-founder of DerbyCon, a large-scale conference in Louisville, Kentucky.

Prior to working at Diebold, David was a VP of Consulting and Partner of a mid-size information security consulting company running the security consulting practice. And before working in the private sector, David worked for the United States Marine Corps and deployed to Iraq twice for intelligence-related missions.

Credits

Executive Editor
Carol Long

Project Editor
Charlotte Kughen

Technical Editor
David Kennedy

Production Editor
Christine O'Connor

Copy Editor
Charlotte Kughen

**Manager of Content
Development and Assembly**
Mary Beth Wakefield

Marketing Director
David Mayhew

Marketing Manager
Carrie Sherrill

**Professional Technology &
Strategy Director**
Barry Pruett

Business Manager
Amy Knies

Associate Publisher
Jim Minatel

Project Coordinator, Cover
Brent Savage

Proofreader
Nicole Hirschman

Indexer
Johnna Van Hoose Dinse

Cover Designer
Wiley

Cover Image
iStock.com/Evgeny Sergeev
and Fishhook iStock.com/Aslan
Alphan

Acknowledgments

In 2014 some life-altering changes occurred for me, and one of the many good ones was my team growing. As Michele and I started to teach my new team members my methodology for phishing awareness, it dawned on me that I had to write another book.

Phishing was being used in a large portion of the attacks we saw in the news, and people are still largely unaware of what phishing is and how to defend against it.

Yet, the clients I was working with were seeing drastic changes in behavior with regard to phishing e-mails—from 80+ percent click ratios and only a fraction of people reporting to less than 10 percent click ratios and more than 60 percent reporting. As the year progressed, those statistics kept climbing and falling in the right directions.

I had just recently finished *Unmasking the Social Engineer*, and I told my wife I would take a hiatus from writing. When I write, I become somewhat of a recluse; my amazing wife describes me as "difficult." I can still see the scene; we were driving down the road, and I thought I would set up my desire to write a new book by talking about some of the recent news stories about security breaches. I started to talk about how phishing was such a huge problem, and I said that I only wished there were a book out there to help people do what we do.

As I paused, my wise and amazingly insightful wife said, "No; not another book right now." I did what every good man would do in this situation and blamed my right hand, Michele.

"Well, Michele and I think it would be a good idea, and plus she will do a lot of the writing."

And here we are at the end result—a documented precision journal on how to master the art of corporate phishing awareness programs. This book will not be covering the phishing often done in penetration testing, where an auditor uses phish to gain remote access. Instead this book focuses on getting your population aware and ready for the phishing attacks that will hit your organization.

There are many people that I want to thank and acknowledge, as this book would not have happened without them.

Again, I acknowledge my wife, Areesa. Thank you for your patience and support and for always letting me blab on about this stuff when you would rather talk about other things. I love you.

Michele, okay, so I didn't make you write most of the book . . . but still without your support this book would not have gotten finished. Thank you.

Carol, you fought for us on this book. I want you to know your effort didn't go unnoticed. Thank you for your support.

Charlotte, working with you was fun, rewarding, and very smooth. Thank you!

Dave K, you know, when you aren't pranking me, icing me, hugging me, making fun of me, embarrassing me, or annoying me with annoying music on the podcast, you really are a great guy. Thanks for your help with this book.

Nick Fureaux, thanks for letting me run ideas by you. Your constant support and advice are why I can continue.

Ping Look, well, if you hadn't spent those three hours talking me down about seven or eight Black Hats ago, referred Michele to me, and kept me grounded, well, this book wouldn't be happening.

My team—Amanda, Mike, Colin, Jessica, and Tamara—thank you for your support and stepping up when M and I needed to catch up on writing.

Robin, heck, who would have thought that after working together for a few years we would be where we are? Thank you for your continued support, friendship, and help. And a big thank-you for writing the foreword for this book.

My loyal clients, customers, and friends that let me run my ideas by them, thank you.

I know from my previous two books that there is no way to please everyone. Some of you will read this book and love it; some will hate it. All I ask is that if you find something wrong, or you see something you don't like or agree with, reach out to Michele and me. Talk to us and give us a chance to explain or correct if needed.

My hope is that you will see the hard work and effort that went into this book, that you will find it not only interesting but also useful on your journey to understand, educate on, and combat phishing attacks.

Thank you for once again letting me in your mind for a little while.

— Christopher Hadnagy, CEO and founder of Social-Engineer, Inc.

No one reads a phishing book just for fun, but my fondest wish is that you find this book both entertaining and useful. A major motivator for me was not only our client base but also the people in my life that I hope to make safer. My nieces and nephews have grown up on the Internet, and it terrifies me just a little that they could already be victims of identity theft before their lives really even begin. So this isn't just a book for security professionals. It's for anyone who ventures online to connect to the world.

As Chris mentioned, it takes a lot of support to write a book. I'm going to apologize ahead of time to the people I miss, because otherwise I'd be at this all day.

Being married to my husband was a major win when it came to writing this book. It turns out he has the ability to patiently endure cold and/or burned dinners while simultaneously doing research and editing my writing. I don't know how many times we had the "Do you really want to write that?" discussion over pizza (as a result of cold and/or burned dinners). Thank you, my love.

Chris, you could have picked anyone to help you write this book. I appreciate that I got that opportunity.

Amanda, Mike, Colin, Jess, and T, you know how hard you work. I do, too. Thank you.

To Carol and Charlotte at Wiley, thank you for making my first book experience wonderful.

— Michele Fincher, Chief Influencing Agent, Social-Engineer, Inc.

Contents at a Glance

Contents

Foreword

Whether you're worried about a hacking attempt at a major business, government institution, power grid, or personal bank, you can always benefit from more information and personalized training in order to protect yourself, your company, and those you love and care about from financial ruin, embarrassment, or worse. At the heart and core of almost every successful cyberattack is the human element. The human element allows the bad guys to identify attack vectors by which to compromise systems. Because the human element is at the core of every successful business attack, Chris Hadnagy has dedicated his heart, soul, and life to helping protect large corporations—as well as every individual he meets—through education and his experiences as a professional social engineer (white hat) and penetration tester.

When Chris and his amazing co-author and training partner Michele Fincher asked if I would be willing to write the foreword for their latest book/education endeavor, I was both stunned and honored. I met Chris a number of years ago as he was just getting his company, Social-Engineer, Inc., up and running. Chris was (and still is) conducting an amazing series of podcast interviews with different experts from across a wide array of fields, all relating to human interaction. From those early days, Chris quickly recognized that human beings are at the core of all cyber vulnerabilities and that technology is ultimately as vulnerable as the human beings operating and maintaining it.

I remember vividly my first conversation with Chris many years ago. I was immediately impressed with Chris's knowledge and passion as a behaviorist. I was even more impressed with how he had combined his knowledge of interpersonal relations, his years of experience working on cyber-related issues, and his talent as an adult facilitator and trainer to large corporations. Finally, it was his sincerity of purpose and his desire to make it all about everyone else that convinced me of Chris's greatness in this field.

Needless to say, Chris and I formed a quick friendship and combined our passion for helping others to create a one-of-a-kind training experience that Chris is successfully running and expanding upon today with his training partner, Air Force Academy graduate, behavioral expert, and co-author Michele. Chris opened my eyes to the fact that the techniques I had been using for years to develop trust with and to lead my fellow U.S. Marines as an officer—as well as confidential human sources as an FBI agent thwarting the efforts of our country's adversaries—were exactly the same techniques that a malicious hacker uses. Through the use of trust-building techniques, the hacker establishes that clicking the malicious link or taking a similar action is somehow in the best interest of the person who received the malicious phish. This is just the type of action that Chris trains people not to do.

I routinely use the teachings of Chris in every aspect of my life as I help others. I also teach social-engineering awareness to government and private companies who are vulnerable to the human factors involved in hacking. In fact, I often highlight a phishing e-mail Chris and I used in our first social-engineering certification class many years ago in Seattle, Washington. Following the week-long training, which included numerous practical exercises where the attendees attempted to develop trust and influence with ordinary people they encountered throughout the day, Chris used the dry erase board to write out a typical phishing e-mail he had been using very successfully as a hired penetration tester. Chris explained how he would typically get about a 75 percent click-through on the phishing e-mail used. After that 75 percent of the population clicked the link, they would be immediately sent to a training site and presented with some material to help them learn what to be aware of in the future. In other words, learning and education became a positive, rather than a negative, event. Following the posting of the e-mail on the dry erase board for the class to see, we used the interpersonal and trust-building skills we had mastered during the week to make a few simple modifications to the e-mail, incorporating three new techniques without adding to the length of the phishing e-mail. The following week Chris told me he had used the modified e-mail and the result went to a 100 percent click ratio. Because of Chris's training, the company he had worked with was measurably more protected than it had been prior to Chris's enhanced anti-phishing training.

What I have learned from that and many other personal experiences since is that Chris is a consummate professional and expert in this area. I—as well as the world at large—benefit greatly from his passion, knowledge, and ability to pass on his expertise so that we can all live much more secure lives.

The contents of this book are perfect for everyone in all aspects of your professional and personal lives. Chris and Michele use their great practical experience as both professional social engineers and penetration testers to illustrate the psychology behind why human beings click what they shouldn't. Combined with Chris's self-deprecating humor and Michele's witty comments, this book is a one-of-a-kind manual to protect your business and yourself while actually enjoying what you are reading. Ultimately, the book is a "how-to" manual on how to run a more secure and prosperous business and to keep your personal life free from the results of malicious hackers.

Challenge yourself, your company, and those you care about most by reading, taking to heart, and putting into place the information this book offers you. If we can take care of the first element in malicious hacks—the human element—the world would not suffer the large-scale compromises that affect millions.

—Robin Dreeke, USNA graduate, U.S. Marine Corps officer, FBI agent/behaviorist, founder of People Formula, best-selling indie author of *It's Not All About "Me"*

For more information about Robin and his services, visit him at www.peopleformula.com.

The thoughts and opinions expressed are those of the writer alone and not those of the FBI.

Introduction

"There was no such thing as a fair fight. All vulnerabilities must be exploited."

—Cary Caffrey

Social engineering. Those two words have become a staple in most IT departments and, after the last couple years, in most of corporate America, too. One statistic states that more than 60 percent of all attacks had the "human factor" as either the crux of or a major piece of the attack. Analysis of almost all of the major hacking attacks from the past 12 months reveals that a large majority involved social engineering—a phishing e-mail, a spear phish, or a malicious phone call (vishing).

I have written two books analyzing and dissecting the psychology, physiology, and historical aspects of con men, scammers, and social engineers. And in doing so, I have found that one recent theme comes up, and that is e-mail. Since its beginning, e-mail has been used by scammers and social engineers to dupe people out of credentials, money, information, and much more.

In a recent report, the Radicati Group estimates that in 2014 there was an average of 191.4 billion e-mails sent each day. That equates to more than 69.8 trillion e-mails per year.[1] Can you even imagine that number? That is 69,861,000,000,000— staggering, isn't it? Now try to swallow that more than 90 percent of e-mails are spam, according to the information on the Social-Engineer Infographic.[2]

E-mail has become a part of life. We use it on our computers, our tablets, and our phones. In some groups of people that I've worked with, more than half the people have told me that they get 100, 150, or 200 e-mails *per day*!

In 2014, the Radicati Group stated that there are 4.1 billion e-mail addresses in the world. Using that figure and a calculator, I discovered that the average is almost 50 e-mails per person per day, every day of the year. Because we know that not every single person in the world gets that many messages, it is not inconceivable to think that many of us receive 100, 150, or even 250 e-mails per day.

As people get more stressed, as workloads increase, and as the use of technology reaches an all-time high, the scam artists, con men, and social engineers know that e-mail is a great vector into our businesses and homes. Mix that with how easy it is to create fake e-mail accounts, spoof legitimate accounts, and fool people into taking actions that may not be in their best interests, and we can see why e-mail is quickly becoming the number-one vector for malicious attackers.

When we are not running social-engineering competitions at major conferences like DEF CON, and Michele is not fighting with students (real story, I swear), we travel the globe to work with some of the biggest and best companies on their security programs. Even companies that know what they are doing and have robust programs for security awareness and protection are still falling victim to the threat of phishing.

We wrote the pages of this book with that experience in mind. We asked ourselves, "How can we take the years of experience in working with some of the world's largest companies and help every company put a plan into action to make the most of phishing education?"

Am I a Builder Yet?

Michele and I started to develop a program that we implemented in a few places. The program is simple but powerful. It involves using the very tools that are used against us to empower us. We know that this concept is not something we invented. After all, there are more than a handful of companies right now selling "phishing services" to legitimate organizations. Many users of those products—large companies—have come to us and said things like, "We have been using this tool for a year, but our click ratios are still super high. What can we do?"

Before I answer that, let me tell you a story. I remember when I was buying my first home. My wife and I were super excited as the closing approached. (We were going to own a home!) So I did what all men who own a home do: I bought some more tools. I went to Home Depot and bought a beautiful set of cordless tools, a saw, a drill, a jigsaw, and some other miscellaneous tools.

I brought them into my house the first day and found the perfect spot on the shelves in the basement for that toolbox. There it sat for a year.

Then all of a sudden I had to cut something. I was so excited; I finally got to use my new tools! I got the toolbox and pulled out the circular saw. I read all the instructions, including something like, "Ensure you are using the proper blade for the material you are cutting."

I looked at the blade, thought, "Yep, looks sharp," and cut my board. It worked. I still had all my limbs and appendages, the board was cut, and the saw didn't blow up. This process continued for a couple hours when all of a sudden the saw started jamming; it stopped cutting. I charged the batteries and did the finger-touch test to the blade and thought, "Ouch, still sharp." Frustrated, I determined the tool was at fault. "Stupid saw; must be defective."

Then a friend came over to help me out. He took one look at the saw and said, "Um, dude, why are you cutting 2×4s with a fine-tooth blade?"

"A what-toothed what?" I replied.

My friend shook his head, and then he gave me an education on blades.

Why do I tell you this humiliating, emasculating story other than to point out my utter lack of manliness? To prove this point: Owning tools does *not* make you a builder!

Phishing tools are no different than construction tools. Just buying the tool doesn't make you secure, and it doesn't make you able to educate others on the phishing problem.

Teaching People to Phish

So, back to the program Michele and I were developing: We started to analyze phishing and security awareness programs and discovered—as many other serious security professionals have determined—that many of them were useless.

No, security awareness is not useless. I'm not so naïve and silly to say that we don't need awareness. But the style and method of aware-ness training just wasn't working. Seriously, raise your hand right now if you ever paid attention all the way through a 30- or 60-minute DVD presentation on security awareness. Okay—the one guy in the back—you can put your hand down. But as I suspected, barely a hand is raised.

People tune out training if it's not interactive and *quick*. Marketers know this; they tell us to make websites interesting, fun, interactive, and to the point. Why should education be anything less?

We started to come up with a plan to make the phishing portion of our clients' security awareness interactive, interesting, and, most of all, not too lengthy. That is why this book had to be written; we wanted to answer a few questions:

- How serious is phishing?
- What psychological principles play a part in phishing?
- Can phishing really be used as a *successful* part of your security awareness education?
- If so, how can a company implement that?
- Can any size business create a serious phishing education program?

We sat down and outlined a book on phishing, defined our program, and formalized our methodology. We then gave a lot of thought to whether we wanted to release this to the public; after all, it took us years of work to develop our method. After we started to see how it was helping so many of our clients, we decided to write the book. On first approach, though, it seemed like a phishing book wasn't of much interest to many—at least not until the events of 2014, when phishing dominated the front pages again and again during real hacking events. Phishing is being used in attacks every day; phishing service providers are popping up every month; and companies all over the globe are jumping on the bandwagon to start phishing education programs.

What You Can Expect

Michele and I hope that this book will help you on your quest to protect yourself and your company against malicious phishers. We want to take you on the journey we went through in getting ready to write this book.

Chapter 1 starts with the basics. It explains what phishing is and why it is used, and we included a lot of examples of the most current and effective phish.

Chapter 2 delves into the *why* of phishing. Why do those phish work? What is the psychology behind them that makes phishing so effective?

Chapter 3 takes a look at just one area—influence—and explains how that principle is used by malicious phishers.

Chapter 4 is all about protection. Now that the first three chapters have covered the bases of what phishing is, it's time to start discussing how you can protect yourself from it. We give tips for both civilians and corporations, as well as analyze some of the worst suggestions we have heard.

Chapter 5 gets into how you can create a corporate phishing program to help secure your folks.

But how do you tie all this information into corporate policies? I know, I know; the word *policy* is like a four-letter word in these books. But we have to discuss it, and the brief but important Chapter 6 is where we do that.

This book wouldn't be complete without looking at some of the most current tools on the market and how they work to complement the program being set up. Chapter 7 covers those tools.

Chapter 8 concludes the book by rounding off all the principles and discussion with some clear-cut rules of making this program work.

Conventions Used in This Book

To help you get the most from the text and keep track of what's happening, we used some conventions throughout the book.

Special formatting in the text represents the following things:

- We *highlight* new terms and important words when we introduce them.
- We show URLs within the text like so: `www.social-engineer.org/`.

NOTE Notes indicate notes, tips, hints, tricks, or asides to the current discussion.

Summary

The idea behind this book is to dissect what a phish is, why it works, and the principles behind it. We want to fully expose all the flaws of phishing so you can understand how to defend against it.

In my last book, *Unmasking the Social Engineer*, I told a story about a friend who is a master swordsman. He learned his skill by learning all about swords—how to use them and how they work—and then choosing the best partner to help him learn how to fight with them. That story applies here, too. After you learn all about identifying phish, become familiar with the available tools, and learn how to choose a good sparring partner, you can then begin to create a program that will hone your skills and help you and your employees, family, and friends stay secure.

Before we can get that deep into the ring, we need to start with some light weights, including learning some key elements such as "What is phishing?" and "What are some examples of it?"

Read on to find out the answers to these questions.

Notes

1. Sara Radicati, PhD, "Email Statistics Report, 2014–2018," April 2014, `http://www.radicati.com/wp/wp-content/uploads/2014/01/Email-Statistics-Report-2014-2018-Executive-Summary.pdf`.

2. Social-Engineer Infographic, April 28, 2014, `http://www.social-engineer.org/resources/social-engineering-infographic/`.

An Introduction to the Wild World of Phishing

Lana: Do you think this is some kind of a trap?
Archer: What? No, I don't think it's a trap! Although I
never do . . . and it very often is.

—*Archer*, Season 4 Episode 13

Because we're going to be spending some time together, I feel I should start our relationship with an honest self-disclosure. Although I consider myself to be a reasonably smart person, I have made an inestimable number of stupid mistakes. Many of these started with me yelling, "Hey, watch this!" or thinking to myself, "I wonder what would happen if *<insert dangerous/stupid situation here>*." But most often, my mistakes have come not from yelling challenges or thinking about possibilities but from *not thinking at all*. This absence of thinking typically has led to only one conclusion—taking an impulsive action. Scammers, criminals, and con men have clearly met me in a past life, because this is one of the key aspects that make them successful. Phishing in its various forms has become a high-profile attack vector used by these folks because it's a relatively easy way to reach others and get them to act without thinking.

NOTE One more thing before this train really gets rolling. You may notice that when I refer to the bad guy, I use the pronoun "he." (See? I even said bad "guy.") I'm not sexist, nor am I saying all scammers are male. It's just simpler than improperly using "they" or saying "he or she" just to be inoffensive to someone, and it avoids adding a layer of complexity that's off the point. So "he" does bad stuff. But a bad guy can be anyone.

Phishing 101

Let's start with some basic information. What is *phishing*? We define it as the practice of sending e-mails that appear to be from reputable sources with the goal of influencing or gaining personal information. That is a long way of saying that phishing involves sneaky e-mails from bad people. It combines both social engineering and technical trickery. It could involve an attachment within the e-mail that loads malware (malicious software) onto your computer. It could also be a link to an illegitimate website. These websites can trick you into downloading malware or handing over your personal information. Furthermore, *spear phishing* is a very targeted form of this activity. Attackers take the time to conduct research into targets and create messages that are personal and relevant. Because of this, spear phish can be very hard to detect and even harder to defend against.

Anyone on this planet with an e-mail address has likely received a phish, and on the basis of the reported numbers, many have clicked. Let's be very clear about something. Clicking doesn't make you stupid. It's a mistake that happens when you don't take the time to think things through or simply don't have the information to make a good decision. (Me driving from Biloxi, MS, to Tucson, AZ, in one shot, now *that* was stupid.)

It's probably safe to say that there are common targets and common attackers. Phishers' motives tend to be pretty typical: money or information (which usually leads to money). If you are one of the many who has received an e-mail urging you to assist a dethroned prince in moving his inheritance, you've been a part of the numbers game. Very few of us are fabulously wealthy. But when a phisher gets a bunch of regular people to help the prince by donating a small "transfer fee" to assist the flow of funds (often requested in these scams), it starts to add up. Or, if an e-mail from "your bank" gets you to hand over your personal information, it could have drastic financial consequences if your identity is stolen.

Other probable targets are the worker bees at any company. Although they alone may not have much information, mistakenly handing over login information can get an attacker into the company network. This can be the endgame if the rewards are big enough, or it might just be a way to escalate an attack to other opportunities.

Other than regular people, there are clearly high-value targets that include folks located somewhere in the direct food chain of large corporations and governments. The higher people are in the organization, the more likely they are to become targets of spear phish because of the time and effort it takes to get to them and the resultant payoff. This is when the consequences can become dire at the level of entire economies as opposed to individuals.

If you move beyond the common criminal and the common motive of quick money, the rationale and the attackers can get big and scary pretty quickly. At one end of that, there might be people interested in the public embarrassment of a large organization for political or personal beliefs. For example, the Syrian Electronic Army (SEA) has been cited in a number of recent cases in which phishing e-mails led to the compromise of several media organizations, including the Associated Press (AP),[1] CNN,[2] and Forbes,[3] just to name a few. Clearly, there have been financial consequences; for instance, the hack of the AP Twitter account caused a 143-point drop in the Dow (see Figure 1-1). No small potatoes, but what about the public loss of reputation for a major media outlet? We could debate all day which consequence was actually more costly. On a positive note, however, it did make all of us reconsider whether social media is the best way to get reliable, breaking news.

Figure 1-1: Hacked AP tweet

Going even deeper, we get into cyber espionage at the corporate and/ or nation-state level. Now we're talking about trade secrets, global economies, and national security. At this point, the consequences and fallout become clear to even the most uninformed citizen. A current story rocking international news alleges that Chinese military attackers have breached five major U.S. companies and a labor union.[4] The companies are part of the nuclear and solar power and steel manufacturing industries. For the first time in history, the United States has brought charges of cyber espionage against another country.[5] All of this was initiated by some simple e-mails.

I guess this is a long way of saying that phishing should matter to everyone, not just security nerds. Cyber espionage might not be something you think about every day, but I'll bet your bank account and credit score are something you do give thought to. My mother *still* hasn't figured out how to check her voicemail on her cell phone (true story!), but she's definitely aware that she should never open an e-mail from someone she doesn't know. Your mom should follow that rule, too.

Now you know the what, the who, and the why; let's talk about the how.

How People Phish

Identifying a suspect e-mail would probably be pretty easy if the sender was "Gimme Your Money." But one of the simplest ways that con men take advantage of us is by the use of *e-mail spoofing*, which is when the information in the "From" section of the e-mail is falsified, making it appear as if it is coming from someone you know or another legitimate source (such as your cable company). Chris and I outline some simple steps in Chapter 4 that might help you identify whether the sender is legitimate. In the meantime, it's simply good to know that thinking an e-mail is safe just because you know the sender isn't always a sure bet.

Another technique that scammers use to add credibility to their story is the use of *website cloning*. In this technique, scammers copy legitimate websites to fool you into entering personally identifiable information (PII) or login credentials. These fake sites can also be used to directly attack your computer. An example that Chris personally experienced is the fake Amazon.com website. This is a great example for a couple of reasons. First, it's a very common scam because so many of us have ordered from Amazon.com. We've seen the company's website and e-mails so many times that we probably don't take a very close look at either. Second, it's good enough that even someone very experienced in the sneaky tactics used by scammers almost fell victim to it.

Chris has been phishing our clients for years (with their permission, of course). He's sent hundreds of thousands of phish and knows how they're put together and why they work. But last year, he received an e-mail informing him that access to his Amazon.com account was going to be blocked. This e-mail happened to coincide with preparations for our annual contest at DEF CON. Now, there's never a time that Chris isn't busy, but the month or so prior to DEF CON is basically all nine circles of Dante's Hell at the same time, in his office. I don't know what he actually thought or said at the time he received the fake Amazon .com e-mail, but you probably know where this story is going. Figure 1-2 shows the very e-mail he received.

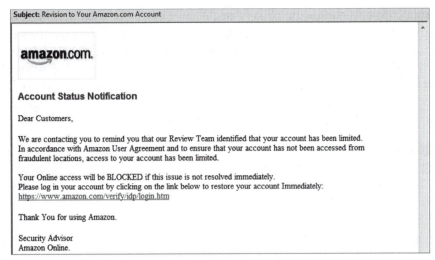

Figure 1-2: The infamous Amazon.com phishing e-mail

If you read this e-mail closely, you will notice that the language isn't quite up to par, and there are anomalies, such as random capitalization. These characteristics are common hallmarks of phish, as many senders aren't native English speakers. The key here is that the quality of the e-mail is more than good enough to pass a quick inspection by a recipient with his hair on fire.

Chris clicked the link and ended up on what looked like the Amazon .com website, as shown in Figure 1-3. Even a close visual inspection wouldn't have been revealed it as fake because the site had been cloned.

At this point, Chris's years of training kicked in. He looked at the website URL (address) and realized it wasn't legitimate. If he had entered his login credentials as he was asked to, his account containing his PII and his credit card information would have been hijacked. This almost worked because the website itself was an exact duplicate of the real thing, and the e-mail came at a time when Chris was busy, tired, and distracted—all things that can prevent critical thinking. (We'll talk more about this in Chapter 4.) The bottom line here is that website cloning is a very convincing way of getting people to believe the phish is real.

One final trick that scammers use is to follow up phishing e-mails with a phone call. This is also known as *vishing* (for voice phishing) or phone phishing. Vishing has many malicious goals, ranging from adding truthfulness and credibility to an e-mail all the way to directly requesting confidential information. This technique emphasizes the idea that you should be closely protecting your PII. I grew up in an era in which people regularly had their Social Security and telephone numbers printed on their checks, right under their addresses, which basically announced, "Please steal my identity, Mr. Criminal!" Imagine how convincing it would be if you received an e-mail directly followed by a phone call from "your bank" that urged you to click the link, go to a website, and update your account information.

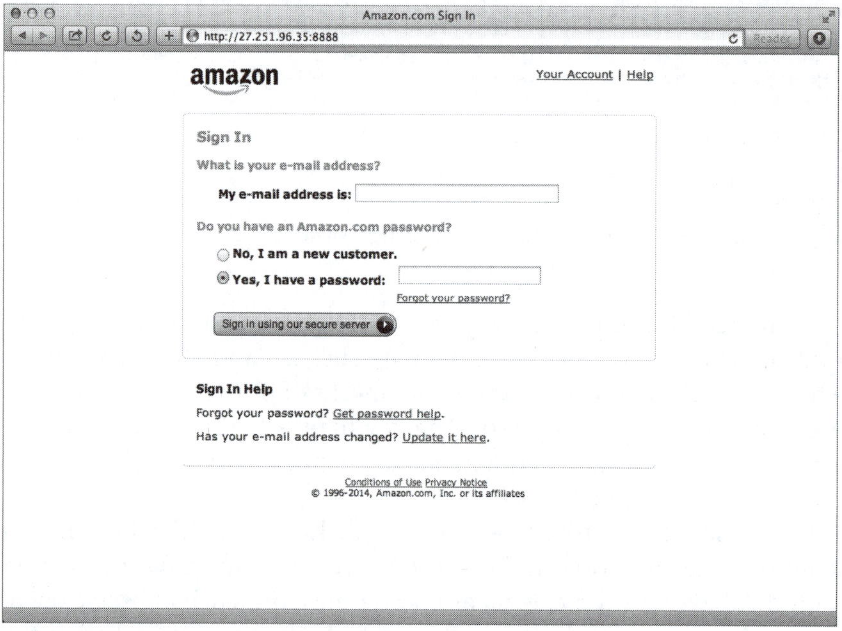

Figure 1-3: Fake Amazon.com website

A real example occurred recently at the corporate level. It was dubbed "Francophoning" because the targets were primarily companies based in France.[6] The attack was well planned and executed. An administrative assistant received an e-mail regarding an invoice, which was followed by a phone call by someone claiming to be a vice president within the company. He asked the assistant to process the invoice immediately. She clicked the e-mail link, which led to a file that loaded malware. This malware enabled attackers to take over her computer and steal information. This example is interesting because so many factors are in play—for example, the use of authority and gender differences in compliance—but the main point here is that any story becomes more convincing if you hear it from more than one source.

Examples

I'm not sure about you, but both Chris and I learn best by example. This section covers some high-profile compromises that started with phish and some of the most prevalently used phish on the market today. We also discuss why they work so well.

First of all, this section would be incomplete if we didn't mention the Anti-Phishing Working Group (APWG—www.apwg.org). We could fill pages about how amazing these folks are, but the thing to know is that the APWG is a global coalition of security enthusiasts who study, define, and report on how phishing is working around the world.

According to the APWG's report dated August 2014, phishing numbers continue to be staggering. In the second quarter of calendar year 2014, there were 128,378 unique phishing sites reported and 171,801 unique e-mail reports received by APWG from consumers.[7] This was the second-highest number of phishing sites detected in one quarter since the APWG started tracking these statistics. Payment services and the financial industry were the most targeted sectors, accounting for 60 percent of the total, but within that, there was also a new trend in which online payment and crypto-currency users were targeted at an increased rate.

Now that you've seen the bird's-eye view of the numbers, it's time to examine some specifics.

High-Profile Breaches

Target Corporation is probably one of the highest-profile breaches to date. It has affected close to 110 million consumers—an estimated 40 million credit cards and 70 million people with stolen PII; with those numbers, you might have been one of them.[8] The interesting thing about this story, however, is that it appears as though the attack wasn't specifically aimed at Target.[9] This is a prime example of attack escalation. Target became a victim of opportunity after the real breach. The initial victim in this case was an HVAC vendor for Target that had network credentials. A person at the HVAC company received a phishing e-mail and clicked a link that loaded malware, which in turn stole login credentials from the contractor. The contractor network had connections to the Target network for things such as billing and contract submission. Not all of the attack details are known, but after attackers had access to snoop around, they eventually found entry into Target's corporate servers and compromised the payment system.

Although the final hit to consumers is still to be determined, the Target breach has already cost more than $200M for financial institutions to reissue compromised credit cards—and that's before taking into account any charges for fraud, which consumers aren't liable for. All in all, this was a dramatic and expensive lesson in the dangers of phishing.

Another notable breach that you may not even remember involved RSA. At this point, any mention of RSA probably relates to the encryption controversy it experienced in connection to the National Security Agency starting in late 2013. That story was so big that it practically overshadows the corporate breach the company experienced in 2011.[10] Unlike the opportunistic Target attack, this one appears to have been a very deliberate action taken against RSA employees. It was apparently the result of a malicious Excel spreadsheet attachment to an e-mail sent to low-level RSA users (see Figure 1-4).

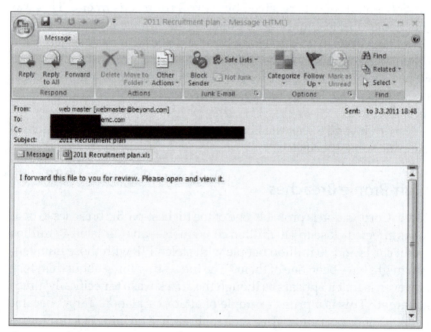

Figure 1-4: RSA phish

RSA's spam filters reportedly caught the e-mails, sending them to users' Junk folders. The interesting point here is that humans overrode technical controls that worked the way they should have. At least one recipient opened the e-mail and clicked the attachment. This gave attackers entry into the internal network and enabled them to eventually steal information related to some of RSA's products. It was reported that in the quarter that followed the breach, parent company EMC spent $66M on cleanup costs, such as transaction monitoring and encryption token replacements.

One more product-based company breach worth noting involved Coca-Cola in 2009.[11] This case originated as a very targeted spear phish directed at Coca-Cola executives with the subject line "Save power is save money! (from CEO)." The e-mail subject line is pretty bad, to be sure, but consider a couple of things: First, the e-mail appeared to come from an exec in the legal department at Coca-Cola. Second, at the time of the attack the company was promoting an energy-saving campaign. (The attackers really had done their homework.) The exec opened the e-mail and clicked the link, which was supposed to lead to more information about the energy program. Instead, he ended up loading a bunch of malware, including a key logger that tracked everything he typed in the weeks to come. This breach allowed the Chinese attackers to gain access to the internal corporate network and mine data for weeks before being discovered.

This breach occurred in February 2009, and Coca-Cola wasn't aware of it until the FBI informed the company in March. By then a great deal of sensitive data had been stolen. This was days before Coca-Cola's $2.4B attempt to purchase a Chinese soft drink manufacturer, which ultimately failed. It would have been the largest acquisition of a Chinese company by a foreign entity to date. There are conflicting reports as to why the acquisition failed, but at least one security organization claims it was due to critical information regarding strategy and pricing being leaked to the opposite side, which deprived Coca-Cola of the ability to negotiate the deal.

As mentioned earlier, the hack of the AP was impressive based solely on the sheer impact that one tweet had on the stock market.[12] The way the attackers got in, however, was a simple spear phish that was sent to select AP staffers from what appeared to be a colleague (see Figure 1-5).

Although this e-mail is pretty vague, consider that it came from a "known" source and appeared to point to a legitimate page on *The Washington Post* site. Victims who clicked the link in the message were sent to a spoofed website that collected their login credentials. There's speculation that the spoofed site allowed victims to authenticate with their Twitter credentials, which led to the feed compromise.

Corporations are clearly as vulnerable to phishing as regular people are despite all of their technical controls and security policies. So what about phish that hit a little closer to home? The following section describes common examples that you may have seen.

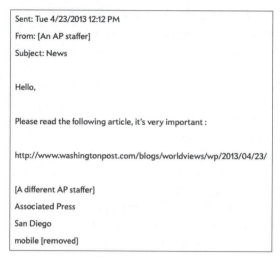

Sent: Tue 4/23/2013 12:12 PM

From: [An AP staffer]

Subject: News

Hello,

Please read the following article, it's very important :

http://www.washingtonpost.com/blogs/worldviews/wp/2013/04/23/

[A different AP staffer]

Associated Press

San Diego

mobile [removed]

Figure 1-5: Associated Press spear phish

Phish in Their Natural Habitat

We would be doing the topic of phishing a disservice if we didn't start with the *Nigerian 419* scam. Also known as the *advance-fee fraud*, this con is apparently more than 200 years old in practice (as you can imagine, it took a lot longer to get scammed over snail mail, but it still happened). It gets its most modern name because of Nigeria's notoriety as supposedly being a large source of these scams. The number 419 refers to the Nigerian criminal code that addresses fraud.

You have probably seen a number of variations of this scam. For example, a rich prince has been deposed and needs your help in transferring his vast wealth, or a dying man is trying to make up for being generally unpleasant and needs your help in disbursing funds to charity organizations. Whatever the cover story, a few components are consistent:

- The amount of money in question is vast.
- They are trusting *you*, a complete stranger, to transfer, disburse, or hold the money.
- You get a cut for your trouble, but you need to do one of the following:
  - Provide your bank account information so they can transfer the money
  - Assist them by paying transfer fees, mostly due to some sort of precarious political or personal situation

Figure 1-6 shows a real example of one e-mail I recently received. Okay, so this one came from a guy in Ghana, but you get the general idea.

Figure 1-6: Michele's Nigerian 419 phish

This is probably a pretty obvious scam to the vast majority of people, but what are some specifics that told me this wasn't a legitimate offer from African royalty?

- I don't know any African royalty—or anyone from the Department of Minerals and Energy in Ghana, for that matter. I don't even know anyone named Johnson Adiyah.

- There's no reason Johnson Adiyah would know me, either. Well, he apparently doesn't, because he didn't actually greet me by name. A deal this big and he doesn't even *know my name*?!?

- Although I appreciate spontaneity, this offer is really, really out of the blue.

- They are entrusting me (as opposed to a bank or a trust or even a law firm) to handle $8.5 million. Just roll that around in your head for a minute. Now, I like to think I'm a generally trustworthy person, but do you know *how much cake and crab* I could buy with $8.5M?

- Finally, although I believe the sender used a spell-checker, this person's use of language is a bit off; it sounds like English is not Johnson Adiyah's native language—which would be okay if I actually knew a Johnson Adiyah in Ghana.

The Nigerian 419 scam really is at the beginner level of phishing scams. It's pretty obviously a fake and easy to detect. You would think that we'd catch on to this particular scam after 200 years. However, it's alive and well and still ensnaring somebody, probably even as you are reading this. Why does it still work?

- **Greed:** It's the first reason and also the most base. Most people will never see large sums of money such as that offered in the 419 phish, and that alone can keep people from thinking straight. There's always a chance that the story is true, right? Well, not really. But if you can talk yourself into believing you have a real shot at winning the lottery, it's probably not that much further to convince yourself that a stranger really would let you hold his money.

- **Lack of education:** We talk a lot more about this factor at various points later in this book, but there is a population of folks out there (which, until recently, included my mom) who have no idea that bad people might try to steal their identity or money through e-mail.

- **Plain gullibility:** There are people in the world that place their full trust in the word of others. It would be wonderful if we really lived in a world where that kind of trust didn't put us in an unsafe position.

Other than someone offering you vast riches, there are a number of very common themes that bad guys like to use. Some of these are good enough to at least give you pause.

Financial Themes

Financial themes are a big favorite of phishers. Most of us put our money somewhere, move it around, and pay taxes, so receiving a notice from a financial institution is typically enough to make us at least open the e-mail. The varieties of phish are endless, and they usually require you to validate your identity by submitting your account details through an online form. Some of the most common financial phish include the following:

- There have been a number of invalid login attempts on your account.
- Your bank has upgraded its online security.
- You are overdue on a loan or paying taxes.

Figures 1-7 through 1-10 show examples of phish in the wild. Most of these attempts are significantly better and more sophisticated than the Nigerian phish; they might contain logos and images, which makes them look much more legitimate. Let's classify these as the intermediate level of phishing scams.

Despite the greater finesse involved in these phish, there are still some details that will help you identify the fakers:

- Greetings still typically are vague; shouldn't your bank know your name? "Valued Customer" doesn't count.
- Spelling, grammar, and capitalization, although better, can still be a little off.
- Links to online validation forms indicate the web address doesn't really belong to the alleged sender.
- Use of urgent language ("Please respond immediately or access to your account will be blocked").

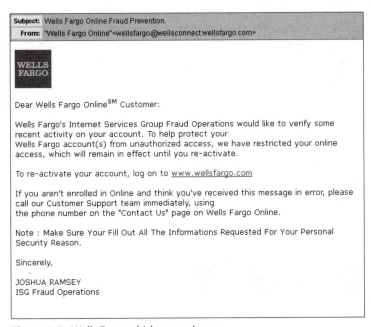

Figure 1-7: Wells Fargo phish example

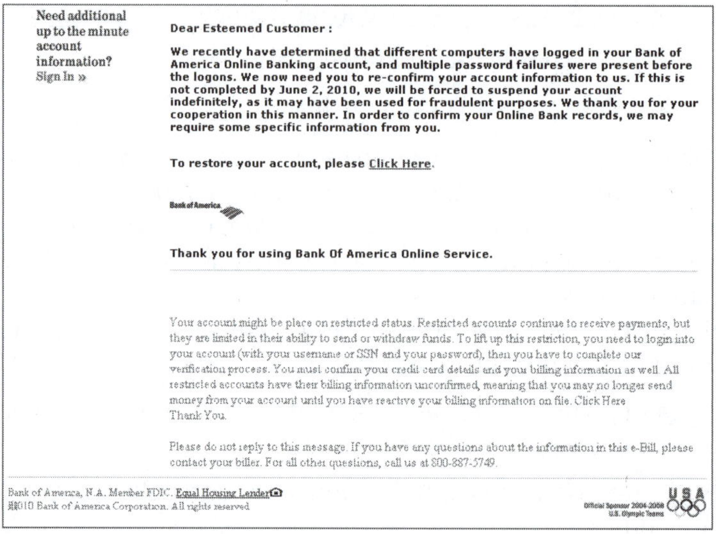

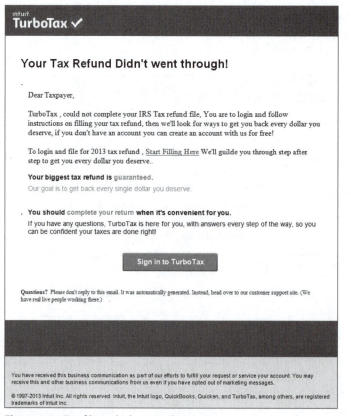

Figure 1-8: Bank of America phish example

Figure 1-9: Tax filing phish example

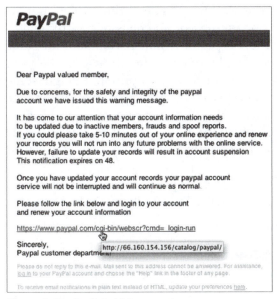

Figure 1-10: PayPal phish example

These e-mails coerce action mainly through a certain level of fear or apprehension. Anything that threatens access to your money is scary. In fact, most of the examples throughout this section have a great many things in common, especially in the way they get people to act:

- **Use of authority:** This is a principle of influence that is covered in depth in Chapter 3, but basically people are social creatures and we all respond to authority in one form or another.

- **Time constraints:** Oh, no! It says that access to your account expires in 48 hours! This kind of language really increases the level of anxiety. Because of our survival instinct, anything that limits access to a resource feels threatening.

- **Possible compromise:** It's truly frightening to think that your bank has detected what could be someone poking around in your accounts. The only person who should be swimming around in my gold pieces is me. And possibly Smaug.

Social Media Threats

Another common theme you may have seen is phishing through the use of social media. Come on—the point of social media is to be, well, social. So getting an e-mail through one of the services notify-ing you of friend requests or asking you to check out a link makes perfect sense. In general, these types of e-mail are at about the same level of difficulty as, and can be identified as illegitimate by the same details as, the financial services phish. In my opinion, though, some of these are easier to fall for because if you participate in social media, getting an invitation of some sort is common and, more important, desirable. In addition these phish might not set off the same alarms that an unsolicited bank e-mail would so you may be less guarded in your response.

Like the financial services phish, these types of e-mails will sometimes use fear to encourage behavior, such as the one shown in Figure 1-11.

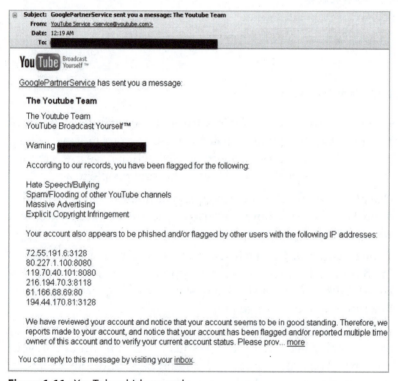

Figure 1-11: YouTube phish example

Fear is a great universal motivator, but losing access to a social media account is more of an inconvenience than a critical event (well, for *most* of us, anyway). However, the social media pretext also gives attackers a couple of alternatives to the use of fear through encouraging participation and connection. These attacks also prey on a sense of obligation. Social media sites grow through the connections that are made. They make participation fun and make you a part of a tribe. Phishing attacks play on those same themes. A lot of people click because they don't want to hurt others' feelings by not accepting a friend request, or they don't want to seem rude by not responding—even to people they don't know. (See Figures 1-12 and 1-13.)

Figure 1-12: Facebook phish example

NOTE You know, I had a sort of virtual relationship when I was a kid. She was a pen pal. I distinctly remember that it didn't have the power or immediacy that virtual relationships seem to have for many people today. The phenomenon of social media is still a really interesting thing to me. It's created a quick and fairly effortless way for people to connect far beyond their typical social and professional circles. Unfortunately, it also makes folks who are interested in meeting people and developing their networks particularly vulnerable to this type of phishing. In this case, it's good to be someone content to live under a rock. I literally have 34 legitimate invitations sitting in one of my accounts right now. I should probably learn to be a little less laissez-faire, or people will think I don't want friends.

Figure 1-13: LinkedIn phish example

High-Profile Event Scams

A final category of phish in the wild that you may have seen is particularly heinous. Scammers send phish directly after a high-profile event, such as a natural disaster, plane crash, or terrorist attack—basically anything that receives massive media attention and therefore is in the forefront of most people's minds. They take advantage of our natural reactions of fear, curiosity, and compassion. These examples are still mostly at a very intermediate level when examined with a critical eye. They contain obvious indicators that they're not legitimate. That said, some people are vulnerable to falling for these types of phish simply based on their emotional response to the situation. And really, what's the best way to keep someone from thinking straight? Incite strong emotion. Chapter 2 talks about an interesting phenomenon called "amygdala hijacking."

Within 24 hours of Target announcing its breach, scammers started exploiting people's anxieties about the status of their personal and financial information. There were at least 12 different scams identified, one of which was identical to Target's e-mail to customers explaining the event and offering free credit monitoring.[13] As shown in Figure 1-14, this phish would have been difficult for anyone to catch. Because the text was an exact copy of what was sent by Target, you would have had to check the sender e-mail or the links. One more thing that made this one really tricky: The real e-mail from Target came from sender `TargetNews@ target.bfi0.com`, which looked dodgy to everyone. Confusion and fear reigned, and the situation was definitely abused by the bad guys.

Dear Target Guest,

As you may have heard or read, Target learned in mid-December that criminals forced their way into our systems and took guest information, including debit and credit card data. Late last week, as part of our ongoing investigation, we learned that additional information, including name, mailing address, phone number or email address, was also taken. I am writing to make you aware that your name, mailing address, phone number or email address may have been taken during the intrusion.

I am truly sorry this incident occurred and sincerely regret any inconvenience it may cause you. Because we value you as a guest and your trust is important to us, Target is offering one year of free credit monitoring to all Target guests who shopped in U.S. stores, through Experian's® ProtectMyID® product which includes identity theft insurance where available. To receive your unique activation code for this service, please go to creditmonitoring.target.com and register before April 23, 2014. Activation codes must be redeemed by April 30, 2014.

In addition, to guard against possible scams, always be cautious about sharing personal information, such as Social Security numbers, passwords, user IDs and financial account information. Here are some tips that will help protect you:

- Never share information with anyone over the phone, email or text, even if they claim to be someone you know or do business with. Instead, ask for a call-back number.
- Delete texts immediately from numbers or names you don't recognize.
- Be wary of emails that ask for money or send you to suspicious websites. Don't click links within emails you don't recognize.

Target's email communication regarding this incident will never ask you to provide personal or sensitive information.

Thank you for your patience and loyalty to Target. You can find additional information and FAQs about this incident at our Target.com/databreach website. If you have further questions, you may call us at 866-852-8680.

Gregg Steinhafel

Chairman, President and CEO

Figure 1-14: Real or phish?

Obviously people with Target accounts were most vulnerable to these scams. Target is such a massive retail outlet, though, that the breach was enough to raise everyone's blood pressure a point or two. Is there anyone out there who hasn't shopped at Target at least once in his or her lifetime?

Chris and I are here to educate, not judge, but the post-disaster variants of high-profile event scams are undeniably some of the most deplorable. Instead of trying to intimidate (which is bad enough), these threats exploit your connection to others. Within hours of the Boston Marathon bombings, scammers were already hitting inboxes.[14] Many were very simple e-mails that provided a link to supposed videos of the explosions. Taking advantage of people's natural curiosity, these links led to websites that downloaded malware. A variant used both authority and curiosity through spoofing an e-mail from CNN (see Figure 1-15).

The worst, of course, are those phish that take advantage of people's desire to help others. Within hours of any tragic event, scammers are sending out pleas for help. Figure 1-16 shows one of the e-mails that circulated after an earthquake and subsequent tsunami hit Japan in 2011. Reports indicated that scams were seen three hours after the initial earthquake.

Figure 1-15: Boston Marathon variant

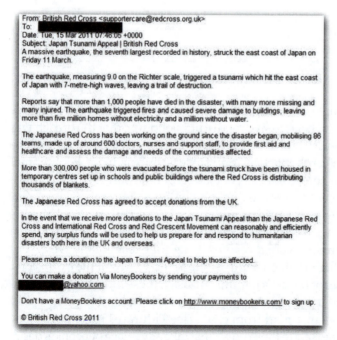

Figure 1-16: Japanese tsunami phish

The example in Figure 1-16 is pretty easy to identify as a phish because the Red Cross accepts donations directly on its website as opposed to taking wired funds through a service like MoneyBookers to an @yahoo e-mail address. But again, after such a tragic and high-profile event, a lot of people were eager to help. Simple phish aside, perpetrators of many of these disaster scams reinforce their stories with phone calls and even door-to-door solicitation, which increases their appearance of legitimacy.

Phish in a Barrel

To summarize this section, phish in the wild come in a variety of types, but some common themes are

- Nigerian 419 (advance fee or identity theft variants)
- Financial/payment services
- Social media
- High-profile event exploitation

The list actually goes on and on and can include any entity that can communicate online (think eBay, Netflix, software updates, and USPS), but you get the drift. Most of these phish can be classified at a beginner to intermediate level of sophistication and have a lot of commonalities. For instance they use the following to coerce action:

- Greed
- Fear
- Respect for authority
- Desire to connect
- Curiosity
- Compassion

Most phish at these difficulty levels have indicators that can help you identify them as not legitimate. However, the characteristics really start to become less obvious when you get to more advanced levels:

- Vague greeting/sign off
- Unknown/suspicious sender
- Links to unknown/suspicious web addresses
- Typos and grammar, spelling, and punctuation errors
- Implausible pretexts (especially with 419 scams)
- Urgent language

Phish with Bigger Teeth

Do you feel like you've taken a drink from the fire hose yet? The deviousness and ingenuity that people use to steal from others is truly overwhelming. Even worse, the previous examples just touch on the most basic phish. There are additional variations that add complexity to a whole new (and depressing) level.

Chris and I started categorizing levels of difficulty in order to help our clients understand what they're seeing and also to track clients' progress in identifying progressively harder phish. We'll get into specific difficulty levels and their descriptions in Chapter 6.

Intermediate Phish

The examples you've already seen are mostly at the beginner and intermediate levels, but some of the examples thus far would definitely fall on the high-intermediate end of the spectrum. For example, the Target letter was an exact copy of the real thing except for links to bad websites. So let's do a little deep dive into the trickier ones and break them down a little bit.

Our first example is another bank phish, as shown in Figure 1-17.

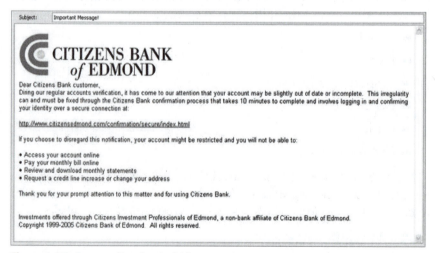

Figure 1-17: Intermediate bank phish

Let's talk about what these guys did "right." What are the things that might have made people click the link in the e-mail?

- **Bank logo**: You probably noticed this earlier, but many of the more advanced phish insert real logos and graphics, which makes them look more legitimate. Because we've gotten accustomed to seeing branding when companies communicate with us, including logos is one way to disguise a malicious message and keep us from really taking a close look.

- **Use of fear/anxiety**: The e-mail states that if you don't take action, your access to your money might be limited.

- **Use of urgent language**: The message doesn't go so far as to say your action has to take place in a set amount of time, but you're certainly encouraged to take prompt action.

After everything we've talked about thus far, I'm hoping the phish shown in Figure 1-17 was pretty easy for you to identify. Did you catch the tells?

- Nonpersonalized greeting.

- No identification of sender.

- Grammar oddities, including unlikely subject line.

- Link redirect. If you investigate the link, chances are that it doesn't go to real the bank website (for example, instead of going to www .citizensedmond.com, it actually goes to www.unknownandlike-lyillegitimateperson.com).

WARNING   By investigate, we mean to hover your cursor over the link so you can see the web address. Never click, and never copy/paste the URL into a browser unless you're a security pro and have a Kevlar-fortified computer.

On the surface, the example shown in Figure 1-18 is fairly similar to the previous bank e-mail, but there are a couple of things to point out that might make this a little more difficult to identify as a scam. Take a look and see what you think.

From: Better Business Bureau [mailto:seatac@bbb.org]
Sent: Monday, April 12, 2010 10:43 AM
To: [Redacted]
Subject: BBB Complaint Case #844383171 (Ref #93-3469167-57423037-6-169)

BBB CASE #866101237

Complaint filed by:	Jason Harlow
Complaint filed against:	Business Name:[Business Name Redacted] Contact:[Contact Name Redacted] BBB Member:YES
Complaint status:	Open
Category:	Contract Issues
Case opened date:	04/09/2010
Case closed date:	Pending

Please click here to access the complaint

On April 9th 2010, the consumer provided the following information: (The consumer indicated he/she DID NOT received any response from the business.)

The form you used to register this complaint is designed to improve public access to the Better Business Bureau of Consumer Protection Consumer Response Center, and is voluntary. Through this form, consumers may electronically register a complaint with the BBB.Under the Paperwork Reduction Act, as amended, an agency may not conduct or sponsor, and a person is not required to respond to, a collection of information unless it displays a currently valid OMB control number. That number is 235-677.

© 2010 US.BBB.org, All Rights Reserved.

Figure 1-18: Intermediate BBB phish

If you looked closely, you probably caught at least a couple of the following details that make the phish in Figure 1-18 a better-than-average attempt:

- **Better personalization:** This was clearly sent to an individual and referenced that person's business. Although there was no use of imaging or logo, the Better Business Bureau is a well-known organization.

- **Better use of fear/anxiety:** This e-mail is a complaint, comes from the BBB, and specifically mentions contract issues *and* the fact that the business has not responded to the complainant. These are all enough to raise alarms with a business owner.

- **Use of authority:** There are all kinds of reference numbers, case numbers, OMB numbers—it all looks really official.

- **E-mail address:** The sender's e-mail address looks feasible; it appears to come from the @bbb.org domain.

Fortunately, there are still some weaknesses with this e-mail; did you spot them?

- The case number in the subject line does not match the case number in the body of the e-mail.

- No identification of sender. Sure, it's coming from the BBB, but you would think there would be a person assigned to be your point of contact.

- Again, if we *investigated* the link to access the complaint, we would find it doesn't go to a BBB-owned domain.
- There are still minor grammar errors.
- There's no such thing as the Better Business Bureau of Consumer Protection Consumer Response Center. I looked it up.

Advanced Phish

Okay, it's time to look at something a little harder to identify. The example shown in Figure 1-19 is an advanced-level phish. Unlike the LinkedIn e-mail shown in Figure 1-13, this one is trickier to identify as a scam. I suspect it is a clone of e-mails you would get that invite you to connect, along the lines of the Target e-mail shown in Figure 1-14.

Figure 1-19: Advanced LinkedIn phish

Why would this e-mail work?

- It's coming from a "real" person. He has a LinkedIn account, so he must be real, right?

- It's social media, so you expect to get invitations from people you don't know.

- It's branded and identical to other LinkedIn invitations you've received.

Yes, the phish in Figure 1-19 is a good one. If it really is a clone, there won't be any indicators in the language, format, or branding that will give it away. In this case you'd have to do a little more investigating.

- Check the links to see where they go (once again, *check* does not mean *click*!).

- Confirm whether the address this e-mail was sent to is the one connected to your LinkedIn account (critical-thinking check).

- If you're extra paranoid, ignore this e-mail and log in to your LinkedIn account to see if there's an invitation waiting for you.

The example in Figure 1-20 is one that a friend of mine received. Getting an e-mail from AT&T was not unusual because the company is his cell phone carrier. Fortunately for him, he's a paranoid security type and thought to check on some things before he reacted. I would definitely call this one an advanced-level phish.

Now, I don't know if the e-mail in Figure 1-20 is an exact clone of an AT&T e-mail, but I can tell you that if it's not, it's *really* good. Some things that probably would have made the average user click include the following:

- Use of AT&T logo, colors, and images

- No obvious problems with grammar, spelling, punctuation

- The pretext of voicemail being inaccessible, which is something that most of us would take immediate action on

So what are some things that kept my friend from becoming a victim?

- It took him a minute, but he realized that the e-mail address at which he received the message was not the one associated with his AT&T account. This was the one thing that really saved him.

- There's no personal greeting in the message.

- The e-mail includes exactly *one* bad link! My friend checked all the links and found something very interesting. *All* of the links except the one link to retrieve the message were legitimate. So if he had not been thorough, this would have looked like a real e-mail.

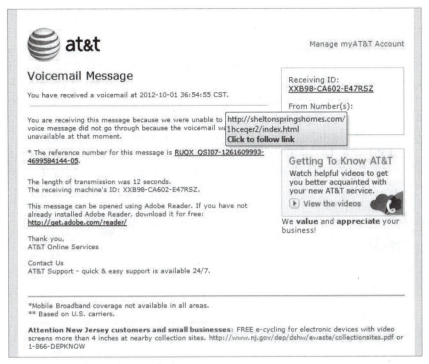

Figure 1-20: Advanced AT&T phish

Clearly the AT&T example is very difficult to identify as a scam; it definitely passes the basic sniff tests. Fortunately, my friend is in the habit of never accessing any accounts through e-mailed links. Hopefully after finishing this book, you'll at least rethink your habits.

Spear Phishing

To finish out this chapter, let's talk about the spear phish. Again, this is a phish that has been personalized to a specific recipient. The attacker has taken the time to get to know you; at a minimum, he knows your first name, last name, and e-mail address. Depending on how important you are, he might know a lot more than that. By doing just a few simple searches, he could find you through social media, your company's website, or anything else that you've participated in online. If you're really important, he'll know all about your hobbies, your interests, and what properties you own; he might even have knowledge about your family. Heck, if he finds anything really bad or embarrassing, he might not even have to disguise his attempt to get what you have. At that point, he could just use that information to extort money or get you to data mine information for him. But I digress. We're talking about phish.

As creepy as it is, it's this level of research that can create a phish that's very difficult to resist. An attacker that really wants what you have won't hesitate to play dirty. He'll find out if you recovered from a severe illness and are now an advocate for that charity. He'll know if you like to gamble online or if you have a mortgage that's too big for your paycheck. This is really the heart of a spear phish. It's personal.

Figure 1-21 is an example of a spear phish that was making its rounds to top-level executives fairly recently.[15] Can you imagine getting this in your inbox?

Figure 1-21: Spear phish

Let's do one final breakdown for the e-mail in Figure 1-21. What makes this a compelling message?

- It uses the U.S. District Court logo.
- It plays on fear and respect for authority. Who is ever happily surprised to be subpoenaed and COMMANDED to appear?
- It's personalized to a full name, e-mail address, business, and telephone number.
- It includes a time constraint. There's a date and time the recipient must appear—or else.

- It doesn't have any obvious typos or grammar errors.

- The sender is plausible: `subpoena@uscourts.com`.

In all honesty, I think this e-mail would be a very difficult catch for just about anyone. The following are only two indicators that I could find:

- The link to the subpoena is malicious. In this example it led to a site that downloaded key logging malware.

- The From e-mail address is `@uscourts.com`, which looks plausible except that the courts fall under a `.gov` top-level domain (TLD).

That's it! Two chances to get it right with a message that's going to create at least some anxiety and the pressure to act. So, once again, unless you have good habits ingrained, this one might have caught you.

Summary

Well, you've now been introduced to the world of phishing. At this point, you should know the following:

- The definition of phishing

- Common targets/attackers

- Reasons people phish

- Techniques used by scammers

- Examples of high-profile breaches started by phishing

- Common everyday examples of phishing

- Overview of difficulty levels

I hope you have a better understanding of what phishing is, the scope of it, and why it's becoming a bigger and bigger problem for all of us.

Let me just conclude this chapter with a few hard numbers. In just a small snapshot in time from May 2012 through April 2013, more than 37 million users reported phishing attacks. That's *reported to one source*, so these are only the ones we happen to know about. It's estimated that close to 300 billion e-mails are sent every day, and of that number, 90 percent are spam and viruses.[16] Those numbers are absolutely staggering, and they really point to only one thing. If you have an e-mail address, you're going to get a phish at some time. It's as simple as that.

Get comfy, because from here on out, we dive into what turns out to be very dark waters. Phishing isn't just about what you click, it's about *why* you click it. We're going to get under the hood of the human OS and see what makes it tick. Sounds like fun, right? Race ya there.

Notes

1. Geoffrey Ingersoll, "Inside the Clever Hack That Fooled the AP and Caused the DOW to Drop 150 Points," November 22, 2013, `http://www.businessinsider.com/inside-the-ingenious-hack-that-fooled-the-ap-and-caused-the-dow-to-drop-150-points-2013-11.`

2. Tim Wilson, "Report: Phishing Attacks Enabled SEA to Crack CNSS's Social Media," January 1, 2014, `http://www.darkreading.com/attacks-breaches/report-phishing-attacks-enabled-sea-to-crack-cnns-social-media/d/d-id/1141215?.`

3. Andy Greenberg, "How the Syrian Electronic Army Hacked Us: A Detailed Timeline," February 20, 2014, `http://www.forbes.com/sites/andygreenberg/2014/02/20/how-the-syrian-elec-tronic-army-hacked-us-a-detailed-timeline/.`

4. Danny Yadron, "Alleged Chinese Hacking: Alcoa Breach Relied on Simple Phishing Scam," May 19, 2014, `http://online.wsj.com/news/articles/SB10001424052702303468704579572423369998070.`

5. Brett Logiurato, "The US Government Indicts 5 Chinese Military Hackers on Cyberspying Charges," May 19, 2014, `http://www.businessinsider.com/us-china-spying-charges-2014-5.`

6. Symantec Official Blog, "Francophoned—A Sophisticated Social Engineering Attack," August 28, 2013, `http://www.symantec.com/connect/blogs/francophoned-sophisticated-social-engineering-attack.`

7. Anti-Phishing Working Group, "Phishing Activity Trends Report, 2nd Quarter 2014," August 29, 2014, `http://docs.apwg.org/reports/apwg_trends_report_q2_2014.pdf.`

8. Michael Riley, "Missed Alarms and 40 Million Stolen Credit Card Numbers: How Target Blew It," March 13, 2014, `http://www.businessweek.com/articles/2014-03-13/target-missed-alarms-in-epic-hack-of-credit-card-data#p1.`

9. Brian Krebs, "Email Attack on Vendor Set Up Breach at Target," February 12, 2014, `http://krebsonsecurity.com/2014/02/email-attack-on-vendor-set-up-breach-at-target/`.

10. Aviva Litan, "RSA SecurID Attack Details Unveiled—Lessons Learned," April 1, 2011, `http://blogs.gartner.com/avivah-litan/2011/04/01/rsa-securid-attack-details-unveiled-they-should-have-known-better/`.

11. Nicole Perlroth, "Study May Offer Insight into Coca-Cola Breach," November 30, 2012, `http://bits.blogs.nytimes.com/2012/11/30/study-may-offer-insight-into-coca-cola-breach/`.

12. Sarah Perez, "AP Twitter Hack Preceded by a Phishing Attempt, News Org Says," April 23, 2013, `http://techcrunch.com/2013/04/23/ap-twitter-hack-preceded-by-a-phishing-attempt-news-org-says/`.

13. Casey Hill, "Email 'from Target' to Customers Is a Phishing Scam," December 20, 2013, `http://www.marketwatch.com/story/scammers-pounce-on-target-fiasco-2013-12-20`.

14. Jovi Umawing, "Fake CNN Spam Use Boston Marathon Bombing as Lure," April 18, 2013, `http://www.threattracksecurity.com/it-blog/fake-cnn-spam-use-boston-marathon-bombing-as-lure/`.

15. John Markoff, "Larger Prey Are Targets of Phishing," April 16, 2008, `http://www.nytimes.com/2008/04/16/technology/16whale.html?_r=0`.

16. Social-Engineer Infographic, April 28, 2014, `http://www.social-engineer.org/resources/social-engineering-infographic/`.

The Psychological Principles of Decision-Making

"I immediately regret this decision!"

—Ron Burgundy (after leaping into the bear pit at the San Diego Zoo)
in *Anchorman: The Legend of Ron Burgundy*

This chapter delves a bit into decision-making. Why do we do the things we do, even when it seems like the outcome will surely be bad? What do other people observe or experience that guides them to make a different decision than you would?

I have a relevant story about decision-making that still makes me laugh. When I was 17, I embarked on my college career at a military school. It was one of those places where smiling was discouraged, and you never had to worry about what to wear—the command staff let you know every morning. Attendance to class, meals, and other events was mandatory. My freshman year, I was fortunate enough to be selected to be in the cadet contingent at an away football game at the University of Wyoming. It was policy that freshmen were to be in uniform at all times, and when leaving the installation, we had to wear a special outfit called a service dress. This was a more formal uniform that included a jacket and billed hat—basically the outfit you've seen on military men in every movie containing enemy threats and secure bunkers.

As we filed into the stadium and found our seats in an orderly fashion, I realized a few things:

- It was a bright and sunny day—it felt like it was about 10,000 degrees—and we would be staying in full service dress the entire game.

- As I sat up straight on the bleachers with sweat steadily trickling down my back, I noticed the opposite side of the stadium was full of guys and gals with long hair and (what looked to me) mostly bare bodies. They were dancing, fighting, singing, smoking, and throwing beer everywhere.

I very clearly remember thinking, "Damn. I made the wrong choice."

Decades have passed since that day, and I'm *glad* I took the path that I did. At 17, I had daily regrets about my choice, but attending that school was ultimately a good decision.

The purpose of this anecdote is to bring to light a number of things you should consider as you read this chapter:

- The quality of a decision isn't always related to our satisfaction with it.

- Decision-making is a sum of a number of factors that include our perceptions and emotions.

- We make large and small decisions every day without having all of the relevant information we might need.

- We make some large and small decisions fairly frequently without any thought at all. (This last one is the one phishers like the best.)

Decision-Making: Small Bits

Decision-making is undoubtedly a privilege, but it can be an awful, stressful thing. Rare and special are the moments that you know absolutely that you made the right choice. As a species, we would love to think that we always weigh the pros and cons of our options and think soberly about possible outcomes. (For example, there's a *good reason* you bought that muscle car instead of the practical hybrid, right?) But you know that's not always the case.

Even though we make dozens of large and small decisions every day, decision-making is a very complex cognitive process that is the subject of volumes of research. There are decision-making models and theories applied to psychology, sports, business, economics, and politics, just to name a few.

I'm not going to try to make you an expert on decision-making, but I do want to introduce a few concepts to get you thinking about it. This in no way represents all of the excellent research that has been done or is being conducted in the area of decision-making. Think of this as a taster.

Even based on a cursory examination, it turns out that there is a host of factors that can affect what decisions we make and how we make them. Before you read what follows and throw your hands up in despair, remember that many humans' (and other species') oddities boil down to one thing: survival. Many of the factors described in this chapter increase the likelihood of survival by encouraging us to think quickly or take higher risks as situations become dire. Although most of us no longer live by tooth and claw, many of our survivalist adaptations have persisted.

Cognitive Bias

I have cognitive biases. You have them, too. In fact, we all have them. Don't worry; it's normal. A cognitive bias is a tendency to think a certain way, often as a result of past experience. Sometimes a cognitive bias is a good thing because it enables you to make quicker or better decisions given the right situation. Many times, though, it can cause erroneous decision-making because it can prevent you from taking in all available information.

If humans were really rational decision-makers, we would make the same decision based on facts regardless of how a situation is presented, but that's just not the case. The classic example is whether you would rather buy meat that is 80 percent lean or 20 percent fat (see Figure 2-1).

Figure 2-1: Which would you buy?

Eighty percent lean means exactly the same thing as 20 percent fat, but the vast majority of folks in the United States would pick the first option. (I specify the United States because in other countries meat is actually sold by fat content.) The *framing effect* is a cognitive bias in which your reactions depend on how a situation is presented. Context matters.

My husband and I often visit a particular web page for the interesting and unique pictures it uses for its wallpaper. One photo was a series of uneven splashes of vertical colors—vivid greens, blues, oranges, reds, purples. Our initial thought was that it was a slightly below average abstract painting. On closer inspection, however, the picture turned out to be a close-up shot of the bark of a rainbow eucalyptus tree. Our slight boredom and disappointment changed to sheer delight, simply because of the new context. The stimulus hadn't changed, but our reaction was significantly altered based on a different presentation.

Another cognitive bias that commonly affects the decisions we make is the *availability heuristic*. This is a shortcut we use to make a quick decision based on what is easy to recall or immediately available to memory.

For example, do you think more people in the United States die from shark attack or by being crushed by a vending machine? Most people would probably choose shark attack, although statistics support death by vending machine. (I know; who keeps track of this stuff?) Anyway, the reason you might have made this error in judgment is you can probably recall news stories and movies about shark attacks very readily, but you don't often hear of someone being crushed by a vending machine. If we can quickly recall something, our brains tend to overestimate its frequency or importance. You can imagine the havoc this tendency can have on accurate decision-making.

One final cognitive bias worth understanding is the *confirmation bias*. This is the tendency to look for or interpret information that is consistent with your beliefs. For instance, perhaps you believe that Doberman Pinschers are a dangerous, aggressive breed of dog. (See Figure 2-2.) If you saw a Doberman barking at the park, you might perceive his barking as hostile instead of playful because of your belief. After going home, you might do an Internet search on "Doberman attacks" rather than "Doberman rescues infant" or even something more general such as "dog attack statistics."

Now, obviously there *are* mean Dobermans, but not *all* Dobermans are mean. But you can see how the confirmation bias can affect accurate decision-making if you're not aware that you might not be considering all the available information, such as the fact that Dobermans are big, stinky babies. (Yes, clearly I have some personal belief systems in play as well.)

Figure 2-2: Is this dog smiling or getting ready to bite?

Physiological States

Are you sleepy? Hungry? Do you need to go to the bathroom? The state of your body can really have an effect on the quality of your decision-making.

Researchers have found that a single night of sleep deprivation resulted in riskier decision-making.[1] They found greater activity in the parts of the brain responsible for optimism, as well as reduced activity in the areas responsible for calculating negative outcomes. What this means is that when we're fatigued, we overestimate our chances at winning.

This concept is something Las Vegas casinos having been taking advantage of for a very long time. From the overstimulation created by bright lights and scantily clad cocktail waitresses to the lack of clocks and windows, casinos get you to stay up late and gamble far beyond the point at which you should have called it a night.

Have you ever been so hungry that you were mad? Chris is very familiar with what happens when I get "hangry." When we're on a job together, he offers to buy me sugary drinks and food about every 20 minutes. But being hungry doesn't just make you cranky; it can also affect risk-taking behavior.

A number of human and animal studies confirm that as hunger increases, so does risky decision-making.[2,3] This makes sense from a survival perspective. Deep down, hunger is a threat (not just an explicit action from me to Chris as my blood sugar drops). Because survival mechanisms are hardwired, we respond to hunger in much the same way that our ancestors did when lack of food really might have been a matter of life or death.

Finally, when was the last time you remember really having to urinate? I mean, you REALLY had to go. Do you remember the sheer effort and concentration it took to hold off? The sound of running water was torture. If you were in a car, every tiny defect in the road felt like impending doom.

Well, an interesting piece of research conducted by Mirjam Tuk and associates seems to support the theory that the self-control you use to *not* pee behind the closest bush "spills over" into decision-making.[4] In other words, controlling the urge to go to the bathroom resulted in better impulse control in areas unrelated to relieving one's bladder.

So the million-dollar question is, "What happens when you're starving, need to pee, and haven't slept all night?" I don't know the answer, but research says that if you eat, visit the loo, and take a nap, your reaction will probably be a little different than it would have been before.

External Factors

The discussion about factors that drive our choices wouldn't be complete without taking a look at our external environment. This includes our physical surroundings and the people in it.

Qualities such as temperature and ambient light don't necessarily have a direct effect on whether we choose chicken or burgers. Similarly, I can't adjust the thermostat to compel you to click a phish. That said, research supports that environmental conditions can impact or intensify our feelings about a situation.

Physical warmth is associated with interpersonal warmth and more trusting and generous behavior, to a point. In "Physical Temperature Effects on Trust Behavior: The Role of Insula," Kang et al. found that brief exposure to warm and cold stimuli resulted in different choices being made in a trust game; brain activity in a specific area is responsible for both the perception of temperature and trust decisions.[5] Williams and Bargh detailed similar findings in "Experiencing Physical Warmth Promotes Interpersonal Warmth."[6] Extreme heat, however, is associated with anger, aggression, and impaired decision-making as evidenced by findings in other studies.[7,8] Think of the nightmarish scenario of trying to navigate a certain resort in Orlando during a heat wave. Not good.

Although we tend to associate sunny days with bright moods, recent research by Xu and Labroo indicates that high levels of light simply intensify whatever we happen to be feeling, and vice versa.[9] So if you're having a good day, a bright room makes you feel even better, but if you're sad or angry, that same level of lighting makes you feel worse.

Finally, behaviors are contagious. Because we're social creatures, the people around us have a huge impact on our choices; we often refer to this as peer pressure, conformity, or obedience. Regardless of what you call it, humans have a tendency to yield to others, especially under certain conditions. Dr. Solomon Asch conducted seminal research in "Effects of Group Pressure on the Modification and Distortion of Judgments" as early as 1951.[10] During the decades since then, there has been a host of interesting research that confirms time and again that our social environment matters.

One of the conditions that affect us is the *ambiguity* of the situation. If I order a sandwich at a counter but have it brought to me, do I tip? I'm not sure. But a tip jar with money sitting on the counter nudges me in a certain direction. Folks in the service industry know all about seeding the tip jar to encourage people to give their fair share.

Other things that can affect my choices are my perceptions of the size, unanimity, and status of the group. For example, did *everyone* tip? Were the people who tipped movie stars and VIPs, or were they regular folks?

I think most us don't like to think of ourselves as mindless sheep when it comes to our choices, but you again have to consider our not-too-distant past. Historically it has made sense for us to conform to keep ourselves safe. If I see everyone else running from the pretty cat with the exceptional mane, I probably should run, too.

The Bottom Line About Decision-Making

Hopefully you now know a little bit more about what affects our decision-making process. Again, the point is not to give you *all* the information and research to make you an expert in what is a gigantic and complex area of study. This is a book about phishing, not behavioral economics. Here are your takeaways from this section:

- We're not always rational and logical decision-makers; there are many factors that affect our choices.

- Phishers understand how we make decisions and try to manipulate conditions to nudge us into making bad ones.

Now that you know some of the things that can affect the choices you make, you can use this information to make yourself and your company safer.

It Seemed Like a Good Idea at the Time

It's probably safe to say that all of us have made at least one bad decision at some point in our lives. This next section is just a small sampling of decisions that could have been . . . better. These examples are mostly funny in hindsight, but while you're laughing, also think about what might compel people to make the decisions they did.

The Heartbleed vulnerability was probably one of the biggest security stories of 2014, affecting, well, everyone on the Internet. Most people's (appropriate) responses ranged from caution to outright panic. One gentleman, however, took the unique route of posting his passwords on *The Washington Post* website and challenging other readers to use them as they wished.[11] Not surprisingly, people did. He provided an online *mea culpa* afterward, but, more important, he learned an important lesson. It's one thing to leave your doors unlocked at night. It's something entirely different to announce it and then challenge people to steal your silverware and your dog.

Here's a question: If you're going to rob an establishment, do you:

A. Disguise your appearance with a clear plastic bag

B. Disguise your appearance with a magic marker

C. Disguise your appearance with duct tape, chocolate, or cookie dough

D. None of the above

This was not a trick question. There has been more than one news story of would-be robbers who, at some point, decided that one of these methods of altering one's appearance would foil detection.[12] Of course, it's easy for me to sit back and mock these guys. They were caught, after all. But it's my (strictly amateur) assessment that they might have made better choices regarding their disguises. What's wrong with the black ski mask? It's a classic.

Here's one final cautionary tale of bad choices.[13] Recently, there was a shop that had several items stolen, including a very distinctive dress. The store used its social media page to describe the suspicious individual and the items that were taken. In a stroke of luck (for the shop and law enforcement, anyway), the shoplifter had taken a selfie in the stolen dress and posted it to her own social media page—as her new profile picture, no less. She was arrested three hours later and booked soon afterward. The lesson here is that if you're going to shoplift, social media is probably not the wisest venue on which to advertise your exploits.

Although these stories are humorous, they reinforce the points I made at the beginning of the chapter:

- The quality of a decision isn't always related to our satisfaction with it. Clearly, these examples were all pretty bad decisions. But at some point, the person involved probably felt optimistic about it.

- Decision-making is a sum of a number of factors, including our perceptions and emotions. What might make someone post a selfie wearing stolen merchandise? Pride? Feelings of invulnerability?

- We make large and small decisions every day without having all of the relevant information we might need. For example, perhaps the gentleman who issued the Heartbleed challenge on *The Washington Post* website did not have a full understanding of the gravity of that situation.

- We make some large and small decisions fairly frequently without *any* thought. Although robbing a merchant is no small decision, the guy who used the plastic-bag disguise probably didn't put a lot of thought into the execution of his crime.

How Phishers Bait the Hook

Let's now bring what we know about decision-making back to phishing. The people who send phish aren't necessarily formal students of human nature, but the good phishers do have an understanding of basic decision-making processes. They know they have a good chance of short-circuiting our logic if they can somehow create strong emotion in us. The challenge is to create a compelling message that works at a distance.

I mentioned the use of emotions in the context of certain phishing themes in Chapter 1, but the following are what I think to be more extreme examples of their exploitation.

The example shown in Figure 2-3 isn't a particularly great phish, but it is a good illustration of the appeal to greed. Would I take $30 if someone handed it to me? Heck, yeah! *The money has already been deposited.* You don't have to make a claim or negotiate; you just have to click.

Figure 2-3: Appealing to a sense of greed

NOTE Bitcoins (BTCs) are a digital currency that translates to real-world money. The value of Bitcoins fluctuates based on supply and demand, and there is a limited number in existence. Using Bitcoins has become a popular way to conduct anonymous purchases because it's done directly between parties without including a financial institution. Coinbase, the company mentioned in Figure 2-3, is one of many Bitcoin exchanges.

Figure 2-4 shows a phish that was circulating around the United Kingdom a while back. The National Institute for Health and Care Excellence (NICE) is an actual medical organization, so this message has the feel of a legitimate e-mail. I don't care who you are; I think you'd be hard-pressed to find anyone who isn't scared of being diagnosed with cancer. This phish does more than produce anxiety over losing access to social media or even a bank account as discussed in Chapter 1. This one calls one's mortality into question and elicits a very clear feeling of fear.

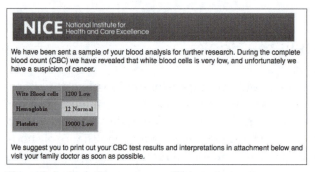

Figure 2-4: Appealing to a sense of fear

As shown in Figure 2-5, the bad guys appealed to a number of different emotions in e-mails that announced the death of someone the recipient knows. The phishers used the names and addresses of real funeral homes. Imagine receiving one of these e-mails; you would probably feel a combination of fear, sadness, and curiosity. This was an emotionally powerful phish that caught the attention of the Federal Trade Commission.

For this unprecedented event, we offer our deepest prayers of condolence and invite to you to be present at the celebration of your friends life service on Thursday, January 17, 2014 that will take place at Eubank Funeral Home at 11:00 a.m.

Please find invitation and more detailed information about the farewell ceremony here .

Best wishes and prayers,

Funeral home receptionist,
Lucas Murphy

Figure 2-5: Appealing to a sense of fear, sympathy, and curiosity

Finally, who isn't looking for love (or at least a reasonable facsimile)? Unless you are really lucky, you have probably made a bad decision related to someone you felt was desirable. As shown in Figure 2-6, life online mimics life in the flesh.

Figure 2-6: Appealing to a sense of desire

Although the examples in this section are all different, the cycle of emotion-based response is pretty much the same, and I would guess that you've experienced this in some form or fashion. In this case, an e-mail comes in, and our interpretation of the message creates an emotional response. This response is reflected in a physical reaction—raised blood pressure, increased heart rate, and so on. Despite our many years of modernization and progress, our bodies still respond to all threat (even emotional threat) as if it were preparing for a life-or-death struggle.

If this response is strong enough, it can affect our ability to think critically about the situation. And if there happen to be any of the factors discussed earlier in play (such as cognitive biases), these e-mails can have an even greater impact. We fall victim to impulsive and emotional behavior. It's a vicious cycle that's illustrated in Figure 2-7. It's also a topic close to Chris's heart, so I'm going to hand the reins to him for the next section.

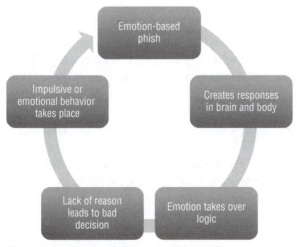

Figure 2-7: Emotional decision-making cycle

Introducing the Amygdala

Michele asked me to step in here to talk about something I wrote about in my last book, *Unmasking the Social Engineer* (Wiley, 2014), called *amygdala hijacking*. Before I jump a few neurons deep into the amygdala being hijacked, let me just give you a bird's-eye view of the amygdala, which is an amazing little part of our brain.

The amygdala is a tiny little mass of gray matter a little south of the hypothalamus and west of the hippocampus (see Figure 2-8). Even though it's small, it has a major job, which is to process stimuli from all modalities (sight, hearing, smell, touch, taste) and send those processes to other parts of our brain to be handled.

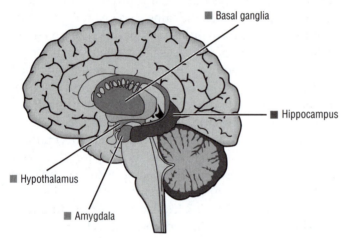

Figure 2-8: Location of the amygdala in the brain

For example, during a conversation with Neil Fallon, the amazing lead singer from the band Clutch, he told me that when he wants to prepare for a show he has a shirt that contains what he eloquently described as "show smell" (and, no, I won't even fathom what that means). He puts the shirt on, and as the smell enters his nose it sets his mind in the mood to get on stage and perform. It's like a trigger to turn on the "stage" version of Neil.

You can almost picture it: The shirt goes on, the smell enters Neil's nose, the amygdala starts to process that stimuli, and it says, "Hey, I know this smell. I need to trigger adrenaline!" Blood starts to flow, excitement builds, and Neil is ready to entertain the masses with his bearded glory.

Here's an amazing thing: Studies I referenced in *Unmasking the Social Engineer* indicate that the amygdala processes these stimuli way faster than the brain can handle, so it triggers a sense of "autopilot" until the mind can catch up.

The Guild of Hijacked Amygdalas

So the question is this: Besides helping Neil get ready to put on another rocking show, how can the amygdala be used? What if a stimulus causes the feelings of fear, greed, desire, or curiosity as Michele mentioned earlier? What happens then?

As the amygdala processes the stimuli and the brain plays catch-up, all goes well if there is a blend of emotion and reason to draw from when the brain starts to activate. But if the amygdala is processing some heavy feelings and emotions, then it has to draw "power" from somewhere, and that somewhere is from the parts of the brain that process rational thought.

In essence, the amygdala shuts down the rational thought centers. When the brain finally catches up to the amygdala, what is left to do the job if the reason centers aren't functioning? That's right: the emotion centers. And what happened the last time you made a decision based solely on emotion?

Here's an example from my own experience: In my young teenage years, I had just moved south and was invited to a beach party in early February. Because I had relocated from the north, I wasn't cold; even though the temperatures were in the 45- to 50-degree range, it felt like summer to me. But all the southerners were cold, and I was tasked with gathering wood for a fire.

The pile got higher and higher until we finally lit it up. Now that we had a nice raging fire, the girls came from the car to sit near the warmth. All the guys were paddling out into the frigid water to wrestle with giant waves, but I kept the fire stoked with all the ladies. I was in the prime spot for a normal 15-year-old boy.

I had no complaints until my friend Matt came paddling in to warm up. He ran to his car and grabbed another board and threw it at my feet. He said, "Are you gonna sit here and be a girl, or paddle out with all the men?"

Now, rational thought would have worked through the steps like this:

1. It's 45 degrees out. They have wetsuits, and I have shorts and a tee shirt.

2. I am from the north, and aside from a few visits to the beach, I have never paddled into waves before.

3. I have never surfed—ever. Maybe a storm swell isn't the best time to start.

4. I may drown; say "no."

Anyone who has ever been a 15-year-old boy, knows a 15-year-old boy, or has read about a 15-year-old boy can probably surmise that it didn't go like that. I worked through the process like this:

1. Hot girls are at the fire. I should stay . . . errr, he just embarrassed me in front of the hot girls at the fire.

2. I need to save face and show the girls I am a man.

3. If I drown, at least I will die a cool death.

I grabbed the board and jumped in the water that was way too cold and paddled my heart out for 15 minutes. I felt I must have been in Mexico as hard as I paddled, but when I opened my eyes I was no more than 20 feet offshore. As I dismounted the board to swim out, my knees hit the bottom. Embarrassed because I realized I was in knee-deep water, I decided to stand up, but then a wave the size of a train hit me and dragged me and board toward shore. Unfortunately, my shorts were still 20 feet out in the ocean.

I was a shivering, very cold (yes, cold water = bad) 15-year-old boy in the nude who had to make another decision while the girls pointed and laughed.

Should I just retrieve my shorts and drive home in shame, never to come out of my room again? No, of course not. I decided I would act as if I didn't even realize my shorts were gone, and I continued to paddle out.

That resulted in 20 more humiliating minutes of pain, suffering, and near-drowning until Matt paddled in, threw my shorts at me, and said, "Grab my leash, moron." Then he towed my shivering white butt out to the lineup.

All the girls were laughing, all the guys were laughing, and I was nearly drowning as I tried to put on my shorts without sinking. And I was sure I could see Jaws coming to eat me. Panic, fear, embarrassment . . .

Finally, I learned to simply lie on my board without it shooting out from under me. I was shivering, cold, and battered, but it felt like I was a real surfer. However, in the glory of learning to lie on the board, I didn't realize I had floated inside the break. I hear people yelling, "Paddle. PADDLE NOW!"

I turn and see all the guys clapping and yelling, and they're doing it for me! My emotions are high; this is my chance to redeem myself. Did it matter that the wave barreling toward me was the size of a house? No!

I paddled like my life depended on it. I imagined that when that wave picked me up I was going to gracefully stand up and ride it like a pro surfer. Instead, I pushed down on the nose of the board, which sent me straight down the face of the wave into the sand bar.

The board splintered, my face ate sand, then rock, then sand. As I felt my legs being bent over my head from the back I had time to think, "Wait, I'm not supposed to bend this way," before I tumbled like a tire down a hill until I landed on the shore break. Again, my shorts had been torn from my body, and the board was broken into at least 10 pieces.

I remember hugging the sand in a prayer of thanks that my life had been spared when I was interrupted by the sound of laughter. I looked up, and I literally had landed in front of the hot girls, this time shortless and also bleeding.

Matt came to my rescue again, walking past and throwing my shorts on my head while saying, "You owe me $75 for the board, loser."

I went home to nurse my bruises. I ended up with pneumonia and a sprained arm, and I also have my eternal memories of humiliation.

Why tell you this utterly humiliating story from my past, which seemingly has nothing to do with phishing? Because it actually has everything to do with phishing.

During my escapade, every time a stronger stimuli was being processed and creating stronger emotions, I was also presented with a decision that had to be made. And every time that occurred, I made progressively worse decisions. My amygdala had been hijacked, my reason centers where completely shut down, and my ability to make rational decisions was replaced with a desire to somehow redeem myself from the humiliation I kept blundering into.

When you receive a phishing e-mail that triggers fear, greed, desire, or curiosity, you stop processing the rational thought that tells you, "No! Don't click that link!" Or "Wow, that crashed my e-mail. I should report this to support." Or "No, I don't know any prince Abu Abu Ali Abu, and there is no reason he would give me $40 million of his dollars." And when an e-mail is actually skillfully written with intent, the emotion it can produce in the target totally shuts down all logic. At that point you make a purely emotional decision.

This can lead us to being totally exposed and embarrassed and experiencing great loss. Sure, I can only imagine a few situations where you might lose your shorts by clicking an e-mail, but you get the point.

When your amygdala gets hijacked, you stop using your powers of reasoning, and you begin to make decisions based on pure emotion. Pure emotion is almost always the worst way to make a decision.

Putting a Leash on the Amygdala

If all of this is part of an automated brain process, how can one fix it? Is there even a way to leash the amygdala?

The answer is that it *can* be fixed; you fix it with time. The amygdala doesn't hijack the brain forever; it is a quick hijack that can be elongated by continually feeding it strong emotional stimuli. However, if you stop and take a moment to relax before you make the decision, you will feel control come back over you.

Here's a situation that you have probably been in (or something similar): I was working with a group, and there was a pretty large pool of people in an e-mail thread. Messages were flying back and forth as the group made a decision regarding how to proceed with a certain program.

Joe and Sarah always butted heads, but they were usually pretty professional. As the thread grew longer, Joe removed Sarah from the thread and said to a few of us, "Who does she think she is? She is a talentless black hole."

As a joke, one of us replied, "Joe, dude, you forgot to remove Sarah from that e-mail."

Joe freaked out. Instead of checking, he just went and sent Sarah an e-mail, including the rest of us, and publicly apologized. "Sarah, my last comment calling you a talentless black hole was unprofessional and uncalled for. I know we don't always see eye to eye, but my comments were rude, and I humbly apologize."

Now, when the rest of us got the e-mail we saw that our little joke had backfired. Someone wrote another quick e-mail: "Joe, dude, that was a joke. You should have checked the CC."

Before that e-mail could be sent, though, Sarah replied, "Joe, since you feel the need to confess your sins I will forgive you, but I am not sure HR will. I am sure you will enjoy communications class this weekend."

Joe quickly read through the thread to see that he was duped. Furious at the "dupers," he clicked Reply and basically said, "You two morons are dead to me. You made me apologize to that glory-seeking, talentless black hole, and she deserved every word I said. Joke's on me, but yours is coming. Payback is a Sarah."

He clicked send, and this time he *did* forget to remove Sarah from the thread. This is amygdala hijacking at its worst. Both times Joe had allowed emotion to take over and cause a very embarrassing situation for him.

If Joe had taken a 30-second pause and looked over what he sent, he would have gotten the joke, had a little scare, and laughed it off. Instead he spent a few days in all sorts of HR training and writing a formal apology to Sarah and the team.

You want to leash the amygdala? Anytime you feel fear, anger, desire, or strong curiosity when reading an e-mail, take 30 seconds to pause. Then think through the steps you know you should take to verify whether the e-mail is real before you click, before you reply, before you take any action.

Sure, the bad guys don't really understand that they are trying to hijack your amygdala, but they do understand that if they can trigger your emotions, they can get you to take an "action that is not in your best interests," and that is the key to social engineering.

Wash, Rinse, Repeat

I know this chapter contained a lot of information. Ultimately, we don't expect you to be armchair psychologists. We do hope that we provided some context, though, for understanding basic decision-making and some of the factors that can make a difference. Will you be able to use *all* of it to redesign your decision-making protocols and be safer at work and home? Ideally, yes. But if you just take one or two points from this chapter and think on your reaction and resultant choices, it'll make Chris and me very happy. Remember: Emotional reactions are normal. You just need to tweak them a little so you're not taking an action you'll regret later.

I think the final point to make in this chapter is to suggest to you that decision-making should be a cyclical process. Chris and I have shared some stories that involved what might be termed "nonoptimal" choices. I'd hazard a guess that most of you can relate to that feeling. As we gain experience (and age), though, we should learn from our experiences and the choices of others. The following five steps (see Figure 2-9) are a way to consider decision-making as something that continually feeds itself so we don't keep repeating the same mistakes:

1. **Make sure you have a good understanding of the problem:** Do you know how you will define a "good" decision rather than settling on one that makes you *feel* good? Do you have all the information about the choice? Do you need to consider other people's perspectives? Have you been in this situation before, and what was the outcome of the decision you made?

2. **Collect information as completely as possible:** Do you have any biases or personal feelings that might affect how you see information? Are you being influenced by others? Should you be?

3. **Consider viable options:** Are there different ways to view the problem? Are there other choices? What might be the outcomes?

4. **Make the decision:** Notice that this is the fourth step, not the first.

5. **Evaluate:** Did the decision meet your expectation? Why or why not? What can you learn for next time?

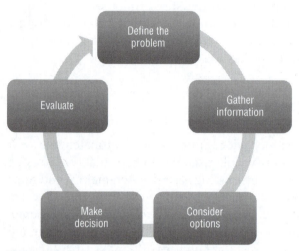

Figure 2-9: Basic decision-making model

Now, obviously you don't (and shouldn't) do this every time you're trying to decide on cheddar or Swiss. But if you get into the habit of thinking a certain way about important decisions, the whole process becomes ingrained and turns into a habit rather than a huge problem to work through every single time. Just take a minute to think before you act. That's all we're saying.

Summary

I hope this has been both an informative and entertaining chapter, but it's only part of the puzzle. This chapter was from the perspective of the decision-maker—the person who picks paper over plastic or chocolate over raspberry and feels strongly enough about an e-mail from a stranger to make a bad choice.

Chapter 3 explores choice from the perspective of the people who write the phish. What tools do they have at their disposal? How do they elicit this strong emotional response that we talked about?

As social engineers, Chris and I need to understand influence and manipulation to help our clients see how they are used against them. So let's turn the lens around and look at the man (or woman) behind the curtain.

Notes

1. Vinod Venkatraman, Scott A. Huettel, Lisa Y. M. Chuah, John W. Payne, and Michael W. L. Chee, "Sleep Deprivation Biases the Neural Mechanisms Underlying Economic Preferences," *The Journal of Neuroscience*, March 9, 2011, http://www.jneurosci.org/content/31/10/3712.short?sid=2ebc4cc4-0b4a-4ae9-9898-7ae10511a01d.

2. Mkael Symmonds, Julian J. Emmanuel, Megan E. Drew, Rachel L. Batterham, and Raymond J. Dolan, "Metabolic State Alters Economic Decision Making Under Risk in Humans," June 16, 2010, http://www.plosone.org/article/info%3Adoi%2F10.1371%2Fjournal.pone.0011090.

3. Phys.Org, "Hunger Affects Decision Making and Perception of Risk," June 25, 2013, http://phys.org/news/2013-06-hunger-affects-decision-perception.html.

4. Mirjam A. Tuk, Debra Trampe, and Luk Warlop, "Inhibitory Spillover: Increased Urination Urgency Facilitates Impulse Control in Unrelated Domains," 2010, https://spiral.imperial.ac.uk:8443/bitstream/10044/1/10464/2/Tuk_etal_PsychologicalScience_2011.pdf.

5. Yoona Kang, Lawrence E. Williams, Margaret S. Clark, Jeremy R. Gray, and John A. Bargh, "Physical Temperature Effects on Trust Behavior: The Role of Insula," August 27, 2010, http://www.ncbi.nlm.nih.gov/pmc/articles/PMC3150863/.

6. Lawrence E. Williams and John A. Bargh, "Experiencing Physical Warmth Promotes Interpersonal Warmth," September 3, 2009, http://www.ncbi.nlm.nih.gov/pmc/articles/PMC2737341/.

7. John Simister, "Links Between Violence and High Temperature," 2008, http://www.academia.edu/443678/Links_Between_Violence_and_High_Temperatures.

8. Amar Cheema and Vanessa M. Patrick, "Influence of Warm Versus Cool Temperatures on Consumer Choice: A Resource Depletion Account," May 1, 2012, `http://papers.ssrn.com/sol3/papers.cfm?abstract_id=2088973`.

9. Science Daily, "The Way a Room Is Lit Can Affect the Way You Make Decisions," February 20, 2014, `http://www.sciencedaily.com/releases/2014/02/140220132004.htm`.

10. Solomon Asch, "Effects of Group Pressure upon the Modification and Distortion of Judgments," 1951, `http://psycnet.apa.org/psycinfo/1952-00803-001`.

11. Konrad Krawczyk, "Man Makes Fun of Heartbleed, Posts Passwords Online, Gets 'Hacked,'" April 16, 2014, `http://www.digitaltrends.com/computing/man-makes-fun-heartbleed-posts-passwords-online-gets-hacked/#!bjg23i`.

12. Natalie Evans, "Robber Who Tried to Hide His Face with Clear Plastic Bag and the Top 10 Strangest Disguises," June 20, 2013, `http://www.mirror.co.uk/news/weird-news/robber-who-tried-hide-face-1966995`.

13. Lee Moran, "Illinois Woman Arrested After Posting Selfie Wearing Dress She'd Stolen," July 21, 2014, `http://www.nydailynews.com/news/crime/woman-arrested-selfie-wearing-stolen-dress-article-1.1874408`.

Influence and Manipulation

"These aren't the droids you're looking for."
—Obi-Wan Kenobi in *Star Wars Episode IV: A New Hope*

You can't really talk about social engineering without talking about influence and manipulation. For all intents and purposes, this is the catalyst for all the decision-making discussed in Chapter 2. As we discovered, people do things for many reasons, but the skilled social engineer understands enough about people to be able to steer the choices made by their targets.

Let's start with definitions. In his first book, *Social Engineering: The Art of Human Hacking* (Wiley, 2010), Chris defined influence as "the process of getting someone else to want to do, react, think, or believe in the way you want them to." Manipulation is much the same as influence, but it is typically described as involving devious intent and almost always being in the best interests of the manipulator.

There's one thing I want to mention before we really delve into the depths of this interesting area. Chris and I make a pretty strong distinction between what we call *influence* and what we call *manipulation*. Clearly they are very similar, and you've probably heard the terms used interchangeably. Both are actions taken by a person that produces an effect in another. But they have a different feel to them, don't they? You've probably heard about someone who's a "bad influence," but have you ever heard anyone use the term "good manipulation"? Despite the fact that both things may result in a decision, a behavior, or an other outcome that seems identical, the way the results were obtained and how the target feels are fundamentally different.

In this respect, I think of influence and manipulation as being at the opposite ends of a spectrum. One end is clearly positive, such as a gentle suggestion given to a family member that helps her make healthier eating decisions. The other is clearly negative, such as information disclosed under terror for one's safety. In between are situations that are much more difficult to distinguish because there are interactions that can have both positive and negative aspects to them. There is no doubt that influence creates anxiety or a need to act; without that, there is no motivation to change behavior. So understand that the point on the spectrum where influence becomes manipulation is not actually a single point but a vast, gray area often open to individual interpretation.

Figure 3-1 provides an example of one way to visualize influence and manipulation. In the figure I added some examples of ways in which they can be accomplished. I expand on these later in the chapter. Using the previously stated definition, it's easy to see why we'd categorize mentoring as influence and the use of threats as manipulation. But there's that large area in the middle. Like all the other examples, however, which end of the spectrum a situation favors depends highly on the choices made by the social engineer.

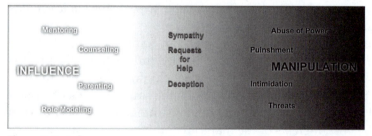

Figure 3-1: Influence versus manipulation

A request for help can be a powerful form of influence or an egregious manipulation. It's one thing for someone to get in the door of a secured facility by asking for assistance badging in, but I think most people would agree that it's a completely different situation for someone to ask for people's money by lying about having a sick child. Does the distinction matter? It does, depending on your goals.

Why the Difference Matters to Us

Chris and I provide professional social-engineering services and education to our clients. These clients care about the security of their companies and the development of their employees. Practically speaking, it's also a much better financial decision to invest in the employees one already has as opposed to constantly dealing with turnover and retraining. As a result, companies don't want their people to feel bad about having been tricked into disclosing information or clicking on a phish. They understand the value of making their people an active part of corporate security. This is much more likely to happen if people feel positive about having been tested and educated and improving their performance. As Chris would say, "Always make a person feel better for having met you."

Can you imagine receiving the e-mail shown in Figure 3-2 and then finding out it was part of a phishing campaign agreed to by your company? The sender is definitely not winning any friends with this one. This was an actual e-mail scam reported by the FBI.[1] When the recipient attempted to follow up, the result was more threats and intimidation.

WHAT YOU WILL DO NOW IS TO TELL ME THAT YOU'RE READY TO MAKE MY ADVANCE PAYMENT OF $20K THEN I WILL PROVIDE YOU THE ACCOUNT OF WHERE YOU WILL NEED TO SWIFT THE MONEY, AFTER THAT I WILL THEN ARRANGE A MEETING WITH YOU AND GIVE YOU ALL THE INFORMATION YOU NEEDED AS A PROVE ABOUT THE PERSON THAT IS PLANNING TO KILL YOU, WHICH YOU MAY TAKE AS YOUR FRIEND. AFTER THIS,I WILL LEAVE THE STATE BECAUSE THE PERSON WILL SEND SOME MEN AFTER MY LIFE.

TELL ME NOW ARE YOU READY TO DO WHAT I SAID OR DO YOU WANT ME TO PROCEED WITH MY JOB? ANSWER YES/NO AND DON'T ASK ANY QUESTIONS!!!

Figure 3-2: Use of threat to gain compliance

There's no doubt that directly after people find out they've taken an action as a result of being influenced by a social engineer that they will feel a moment of embarrassment or irritation. But that's likely to be a lot worse and a lot harder for a company to manage if they felt forced into an action as a result of terror, rage, or shame. That type of environment is just not conducive to learning. You can also imagine how destructive this can be toward the investment an employee is willing to make in the company. That's why we emphasize the distinction between influence and manipulation. It's not just that we're nice people. We're educators as well, and knowing the difference between influence and manipulation makes good educational sense.

How Do I Tell the Difference?

We hope being able to make the distinction between influence and manipulation matters to you as much as it does to us. I'll be the first to admit, though, that the gray area can be tricky. So the following sections cover questions we ask ourselves when we're getting ready for an engagement.

How Will We Build Rapport with Our Targets?

In some sources, *rapport* has a long and complicated definition. It's something that's easy to understand and recognize, but it's a bit harder to define in a concise sentence. Basically, rapport is the ability to build a relationship with another person, and it includes elements such as mutual liking and comfort. Establishing rapport is a skill that successful social engineers must build quickly in order to be effective. Rapport is one of the necessary conditions of influence. When you've established rapport, people will comply with your request because they like you, they feel a connection with you, and they want to help.

The existence of rapport is unlikely and unnecessary for people who are using manipulation. A person who's willing to use threats against someone to obtain compliance probably doesn't really care about having any kind of connection with him. In fact, the less of a connection the manipulator has, the better. Frankly, it's very hard for most people to use manipulation tactics on those they feel a personal connection to.

How Will Our Targets Feel After They Discover They've Been Tested?

The counselor in me always wants to ask this question: "You've clicked on my phish; how does that make you feel?" As I discussed earlier, feelings of embarrassment or even irritation can still lead to teachable moments. You've placed a challenge in front of your targets and they came up short, which could ultimately expose them or their company to a threat. But if you follow up with the information the person needs to succeed the next time, you've created a learning-based environment. Hopefully over time, you can create a corporate culture that moves beyond embarrassment to one in which people are eagerly awaiting their next training challenge. We've seen it happen!

On the other hand, if you have used methods that gained compliance through inciting fear, rage, shame, or powerlessness, chances are that the teachable moments will be lost in the avalanche of backlash you're likely to experience. People will remember the way you made them feel—not the lesson.

What Is Our Intent?

I'm not talking about the obvious and pretty stuff that sounds good in front of a customer. I'm talking about the intent that speaks to your ego and your personal needs. Do you really care whether your organization learns and improves? Or do you just want to feel like you won the engagement because you got people to do something they shouldn't? This is a personal question that you need to answer for yourself. Most of us like the feeling of winning, and sometimes a social-engineering engagement can start to feel like a game.

Fortunately, there are times when you can win *and* serve your company well. But there may come a time during an engagement when you haven't gotten any flags and your ego is starting to take a beating. You also may be feeling anxious about giving the management something for its money. That's when you really have to question your choices and your motives because the temptation to use manipulative tactics may be very strong. Chances are, if you truly have your company's best interests at heart, you'll make the appropriate decision.

But the Bad Guys *Will* Use Manipulation . . .

One question or comment we always get is regarding why we don't use manipulation. After all, the bad guys most certainly *will*. It's a legitimate question. The bad guys want to win. They don't care about their victims, and they're not concerned about teachable moments. Frankly, manipulation works, and it's easy. However, in addition to being more damaging than useful in a professional context, using manipulation is just not a good long-term choice.

After someone has been manipulated, it's unlikely that she will ever comply with another request from you again. This may be acceptable or even desirable, depending on your job and your goals. But in the world of corporate security and associated professional relationships, this isn't the optimal choice because you're looking to build long-term relationships.

I agree that the unwillingness to step over this line results in testing and education that's not as realistic as it could be, but I also don't need to leap into a volcano to know that it really hurts. Corporate security goals can absolutely be accomplished without having to resort to terrifying or enraging the employees. In the hands of a skilled professional social engineer, the experience provided can be challenging without being damaging.

Lies, All Lies

So let's chat a little bit about some of the examples shown in Figure 3-1. One that always grabs people's attention is *deception*. People feel a certain way about lying, and the idea of it is definitely tinged with negative affect. Clearly, if someone yells "You're a liar!" at you, then he is not giving you a compliment.

However, most people want to attach moral and ethical value to this concept independent of any context, and I think that's problematic. The question is not whether you will use deception as a part of a social-engineering engagement. You definitely will.

For me, the question comes down to intent and motive. If my husband has already eaten two candy bars and half a package of cookies, and I tell him we don't have any rice pudding when the truth is that I've hidden it, I'm telling a fib out of concern for his health. On the other hand, hiding the rice pudding and lying about it so I can have it for myself . . . well, that's just mean. Notice, in this example I have the *exact same action and outcome regardless of my motive, but the resultant feeling my husband would have if he ever found out would be very different.* (By the way, the rice pudding? It was delicious.)

The concept of lying has a bad rap, but there's no doubt that all of us do it, to greater and lesser degrees. We are social animals and getting along in groups simply means being smart about what we say (or don't say). Think about how different your relationships would be if you were entirely honest about your friend's grooming habits, your mom's taste in furniture, or your significant other's level of fitness. The truth can hurt.

Humans and other species appear to have an innate propensity for deception. There are a number of fascinating studies that indicate that babies have this ability even before they're verbal. I imagine if any of you out there are parents, you can confirm this. Dr. Vasudevi Reddy from the University of Portsmouth found that well before babies speak—or, more important, have the cognitive ability to fully understand concepts like "the truth"—they engage in behaviors that deceive others.[2]

I clearly remember my younger brother employing the "fake crying" scenario when he was a baby. He wasn't hungry or uncomfortable, and he didn't need to be changed. But he'd often stand up in his playpen and utter an unenthusiastic "Waaahhh. . . ?" followed by seconds of looking around to see who heard. Not the most sophisticated play, but it did get him some attention. From the time that we're small, we look for ways to engage in social interactions. Like any other organism, we'll continue to behave in certain ways if we're reinforced. Deception is an adaptive form of social behavior, and it doesn't always need to be considered negative.

P Is for Punishment

Another of the examples I listed in Figure 3-1 is punishment. In behavioral psychology, *punishment* is defined as a consequence that decreases the chances that a behavior will recur in the future. In this context, an example would be putting your child in time-out for, say, lying.

For the purposes of this book, though, I'm talking about punishment between adults that results in some sort of manipulative outcome. So, parents, I'm not accusing you of manipulation. This is a different beast.

In the social-engineering context, punishment is an interaction between adults that compels the target into desired behaviors as a result of negative consequences. The difference is the apparent target versus the actual target. The interesting thing about punishment is that it's a direct action on a person, but the effect is often to control and determine others' behavior. It's certainly possible to change another adult's behavior by punishing him or her, but at that point, it's not really sneaky manipulation; rather it's simply behavior leading to consequence. You yell at me; I punch you. No more yelling.

Manipulation through punishment can act as a catalyst or create a link to other strong emotions that compel behavior, as illustrated in Figure 3-3. When a punishment is carried out in public, the punisher has created an audience of witnesses waiting for the outcome. Depending on individual differences, they may react with fear, anger, or sympathy.

There's no doubt that some people react to punishment with indifference or avoidance. But if punishment is severe enough, it *will* get a reaction. And that's exactly what a malicious attacker is looking for and seeks to control.

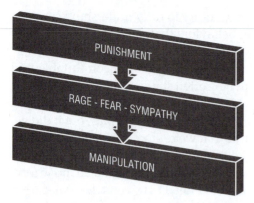

Figure 3-3: Punishment as a manipulation tactic

Imagine walking into the cafeteria at work and seeing a male verbally attacking and abusing a weeping female co-worker. (She might look like the woman in Figure 3-4.) After the attacker storms off, the victim tearfully turns to you and shares that her boss is threatening to fire her because she's forgotten her badge at home. She needs to get to the executive floors of the building so she can complete her updates for HR. Would you help?

Figure 3-4: Would you help this woman?

You may be savvy enough to walk her all the way to security for a new badge, or you may be just angry enough at what you saw to badge her onto the executive elevator. Now *that's* manipulation.

Principles of Influence

Now that you understand a little bit about our distinction between influence and manipulation, it's time to spend some time diving deeper into influence to see how and why certain things work. There are a number of people who do outstanding research in the field of influence, including Dr. Robert Cialdini, Dr. Allan Cohen, and Dr. David Bradford. I invite you to review their work.

> **NOTE** If you'd like to read more about the research on influence, try the following resources:
>
> ▪ Robert Cialdini, *Influence: The Psychology of Persuasion,* Revised Edition (Harper Business, 2006)
>
> ▪ Allan R. Cohen and David L. Bradford, *Influence Without Authority* (Wiley, 2005)

Figure 3-5 provides a quick roll up of the principles as we employ them based on some of this research, as well as on our own experience from our social-engineering engagements. There are some things you should note here:

- Because human behavior doesn't tend to be neat and tidy, many of these principles work together, and you can see the interactions in the examples.

- Some of the examples are applicable to more than one aspect of influence.

- Because the examples are ones we've seen in the real world, many explain how the principle was exploited to manipulate people. (Remember that big gray area between influence and manipulation I mentioned earlier?)

- The "pro tips" are intended to provide you with a deeper understanding and application of the principle, something that's important if you will be providing services to make your organizations more secure.

Reciprocity

Definition: Reciprocity is the pervasive belief that people should be paid back for what they do. The old adages of "One good turn deserves another" and "An eye for an eye" are ways of stating reciprocity. The concept is so powerful that Cohen and Bradford consider it to be the basis for *every* form of influence.[3]

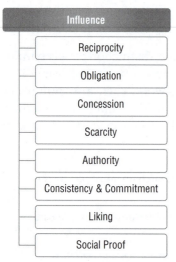

Figure 3-5: Principles of influence

Example: An example of a real-world exploitation of this principle is a scam that offers refunds in exchange for personal information.[4] The key here is that the malicious attacker makes it seem like the target is getting something *first* (the refund). Because the target feels like he's been given a gift of sorts, he feels the need to reciprocate with something (personal information).

Pro tip: Although the principle of reciprocity is based on a gift, consider that the gift doesn't have to be material. It could be a smile, a sympathetic ear, even opening a door first. It just needs to be valuable to the recipient in order to have the power to create influence.

Obligation

Definition: While reciprocity is based on a gift, *obligation* creates influence through things like customs, manners, feelings, and roles. When someone lets me into traffic, I really feel a sense of pressure to give the "obligatory wave." It's just polite. Have you ever been on the flip side and let in someone who *didn't* give the wave? How rude!

Example: A real-world exploitation of how obligations create influence is the horrible grandparent scam.[5] Fraudsters pretending to be grandkids who are in trouble call seniors. Typically, the caller requests secrecy and says money is needed to get out of jail. Many of the scammers will have done research and know things about their targets, such as any nicknames they use. They prey on roles and feelings these poor folks have. It's like one victim said, "You don't want any harm to your grandchild."

Pro tip: How do you create a sense of obligation in people you don't know? How about appealing to something about their identity? Are they a parent? Do they think of themselves as good Samaritans? After you identify something, you can use that as a theme to create a need to assist you and/or behave in a way that is consistent with how the other person views herself.

Concession

Definition: Have you ever had a fight with a significant other that ended in a stalemate? The result might be a day full of lots of chilly glances and monosyllabic answers. What do you suppose is the one way you know you've won? (Ladies, I'm going to say that when your partner shuffles into the living room, sits down next to you, and says, "So, uh, what's for dinner?" you know you've got him.) *Concession* is when one person yields. It's usually an indicator that power has shifted from the one who yields.

The reason why this matters is that concession places the target in a difficult situation. Human nature is such that after people yield, they are much more likely to continue to do so. This is also known as the "foot-in-the-door technique." Think about people who are trying to sell stuff by handing out fliers. They know if they can get you to take the flier, you'll probably at least stick around for the sales pitch.

Example: The grandparent scam works as an illustration of concession, in addition to being an example of obligation. In one particular case, a grandmother was scammed out of $20,000—but not all at once. After the victim had yielded once and provided money, the scammers continued to make requests for additional money, and she ended up complying.[6]

Pro tip: The professional social engineer sometimes guides the interaction by being the one who yields. Through this action, the social engineer implies that power has been granted to the target, although the concession may have been minimal or meaningless. Car salesmen do this all the time.

Scarcity

Definition: Resources are more valuable when they are rare or dwindling. This is another one of those reactions that's hardwired in us. There was a time when *not* grabbing the last chicken wing really was a matter of survival, not just one that provided a sense of satisfaction of denying it to your sibling.

Here's the real irony. I live and breathe this stuff. I totally understand the mechanisms underlying *scarcity*. But when I see ads that say, "YOU'LL *NEVER* SEE THESE PRICES AGAIN!" I sometimes buy what's advertised. In fact, sometimes I buy two.

Example: Where to begin with this one? You see real scams and ads that are practically scams almost every day. In the 1970s, a nightclub owner named Steve Rubell created crazy demand for his nightclub simply by erecting a velvet rope and allowing only certain folks in. There's a commercial for a gold coin *replica* (ostensibly *not* a scam) that actually states, "Avoid disappointment and future regret."

Pro tip: Like reciprocity, the resource that's rare or dwindling doesn't have to be a material object. Have you ever tried to make an appointment with someone important? Does she really have only 10 minutes next Thursday at 1:20? How does the implied scarcity affect your sense of urgency and behaviors?

Authority

Definition: *Authority* is the power to make decisions. This power can come from legal or other legitimate sources, or it can have its basis in personal charisma or credibility.

Example: We grow up listening to and rebelling against authority. By the time we're adults, we tend to react automatically to persons and symbols of authority. If there's a guy in a hard hat and safety vest waving you to a different lane of traffic, you'll probably comply.

An especially egregious exploitation of this principle was experienced by a number of fast-food restaurants. A caller identifying himself as a law enforcement official spoke to restaurant managers, saying that a specific employee had been stealing or dealing drugs.[7] The managers were typically directed to lock the employee in a back room, strip-search him or her, and otherwise humiliate these folks while the caller was on the line. As you can tell from this example, authority has a high propensity for abuse and can easily be used as a manipulation.

Another interesting example was one in which a woman impersonating the manager of a Waffle House entered the business, did some cursory inspections, and then took money from the cash register.[8] She simply acted like she belonged there: according to police, "There was no intimidation made nor was there a weapon used."

Pro tip: You don't have to wave a badge to project authority. Dress, speaking and writing style, body language, and signature blocks in an e-mail can convey that you know what you're talking about and deserve to be requesting compliance. Here's a non-PC tip for ladies: In-person projection of authority can be a challenge depending on your physical appearance and other qualities, such as age and voice pitch. Be aware of what you're projecting, work on what you can, and be careful in your pretext selection.

Consistency and Commitment

Definition: *Consistency and commitment* pertain to the concept that after people have stepped over a behavioral boundary and started down a path, they are more inclined to complete their chosen course of action. As you might have surmised, it goes hand in hand with the principle of concession. After a person has yielded, consistency and commitment ensure the person feels pressure to continue to yield. People like to behave consistently. How do you feel about someone who's always changing his mind? No one wants to be thought of as that guy.

Example: There was one report of a woman who was scammed via the Christian Mingle dating site.[9] The interesting thing about this story is that both the victim and the perpetrator demonstrated the need for consistency and commitment. The victim, like many victims, demonstrated her commitment by cleaning out her bank account for her suitor over a period of time. The perpetrator also went to great lengths to appear to be a consistently loving partner by e-mailing messages and plans for the future almost every day.

Pro tip: After people comply with a request, they are likely to continue to do so. Experienced social engineers are able to continue escalation without it seeming odd or overly intrusive while managing their own personal discomfort with continuing to ask for favors. This concept of escalation was stunningly highlighted during Dr. Stanley Milgram's experiments in the 1960s.[10]

Although the purpose of the study was to determine how far people would go to obey an authority figure, it was also a great illustration of the concept of escalation. The participant was asked to "teach" the memorization of word pairs to a learner through the application of (fake) electric shocks. Each time the learner made a mistake, the teacher was to increase the intensity of the shock by 15 volts. Figure 3-6 shows a picture of the panel that participants saw.

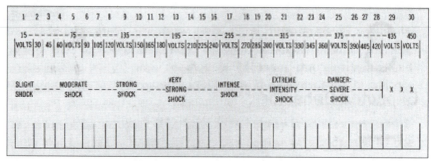

Figure 3-6: Milgram's "shock" panel

Imagine yourself in the position of teacher. First, you have agreed to participate in an important study. Second, you have agreed to the conditions of the study. Then, you do it. You issue your first shock at 15 volts. Although that doesn't seem too bad, your learner continues to make mistakes, making it necessary for you to administer higher and higher voltages. At some point, you start to become uncomfortable. There's a huge difference between 15 and 150 volts, but somehow, you've crept up to it. How do you stop? When do you stop? If you stop, will it mess up the experiment? Can you deal with being a quitter?

Again, Milgram was studying people's obedience to authority figures, but you can see how much pressure consistency and commitment place on the individual.

Liking

Definition: Have you ever met someone you liked right away? Aside from the person's ability to establish immediate rapport (pro tip!), what do you think was the reason you liked the person? We tend to like people who like us. And we *really* like people who are like us. Advertisers use this principle all the time by hiring actors that we either admire (and want to emulate) or can relate to.

Example: Unfortunately, malicious attackers often use our desire to help the people we like. The classic "stranded traveler" phish works because the scammers compromise a person's e-mail and then contact friends and family as the victim needing money.[11]

Pro tip: So, how in the world do you get someone to like you immediately? Professional social engineers work on their abilities to establish quick rapport by developing qualities such as active listening skills and nonverbal behavior that's consistent with what they say. Another simple way to increase *liking* is to identify genuine similarities between you and your target. When you have things in common with someone, it makes it harder to say no.

Social Proof

Definition: I have a very real dilemma. I sometimes go to restaurants where I order at a counter, but then I sit at a table and wait for someone to bring my food and drink to me. Should I tip? I'm not sure. Something that always inspires me to tip is the sight of a tip jar on the counter, which is social proof in action. *Social proof* is our natural tendency to look to others to guide our own behavior. This effect is especially strong in ambiguous situations like my little tipping scenario.

Example: Social proof is an extremely powerful principle of influence because of our social nature. We think, "It must be the right thing to do if everyone else is doing it." Scammers have always taken advantage of this tendency, but now that we're so connected via the Internet, and especially social media, it becomes an even bigger problem. As mentioned in Chapter 1, post-disaster scams tend to blow up quickly because people want to help. These scams tend to circulate quickly on social media[12] and give the illusion that everyone is sending money via certain avenues.

Pro tip: Social engineers often create the illusion of social proof to encourage behavior. Surveys and petitions that have been completed by others make it more comfortable to provide your own information. People gathered around a discussion make it almost impossible for others to walk by without at least taking a peek and a listen.

More Fun with Influence

Social proof is a great segue for this next section because it explains a little more about why the principles of influence work. The bottom line is that they all hinge on our social nature as human beings, but there are other factors that affect the effectiveness of influence.

Our Social Nature

What in the world does being social have to do with influence? Just about everything, really. Before modern science came along and assisted in the survival of both strong and weak, humans relied on the shelter and comfort of others against a hostile world. Aside from a few notable exceptions, the guy who decided to strike out on his own . . . well . . . died, along with his genetic material. The ultimate penalty for ancient peoples was to be cast out of the tribe. So being sensitive to one's social environment wasn't just a nicety; it was the best chance to survive and reproduce.

Over the years, this has become a part of our nature. We are essentially hardwired to respond to both overt and subtle group demands. So instead of blaming teens for caving to peer pressure or calling people stupid for brainlessly following the crowd, understand that they're reacting with instinctive survival behavior.

Pro tip: In modern times, social engineers use the knowledge of our social natures to create conditions that mimic group pressure. Even "lone wolves" likely feel some social pressure to behave in certain ways, depending on the circumstances and people in the situation. Social engineers basically manufacture situations to create a certain level of tension, anxiety, or motivation to act. The best of us do it in very organic ways that feel very natural. That's the real trick for social engineers— making a contrived situation feel like a genuine interaction between two (or more) individuals.

Physiological Response

Chris talked about the role the amygdala plays in emotional versus rational thinking in Chapter 2. When the brain is hit with certain stimuli, there's a whole bunch of really interesting things that happen to the body as well. Although it's really not proper to separate what happens in the brain from what happens in the body from what happens psychologically, I'm pretty much going to do that now.

If a threat is perceived, the amygdala starts a cascading series of events that prepare the human for survival. Regardless of whether the threat is a shark preparing to eat your face or an e-mail claiming that you have cancer, your body reacts the same way.

Your autonomic nervous system dumps stress hormones into your body, increasing your heart rate and blood pressure, dilating your pupils, and shunting blood flow to major muscle groups.[13] These physiological changes get the body ready for action. What's important to know about this is that there is an optimal level of arousal for best performance (including cognitive performance).[14]

Pro tip: This implies that if social engineers are able to impact and control the stress levels of their targets, they actually have a shot at affecting the quality of their decision-making. Combine this with some other factors, such as behaviors that create certain psychological responses, and you have influence.

Psychological Response

What are some of these psychological responses of which I speak? For one, our nonverbal behavior has a significant impact on other people. One of the ways you can almost guarantee putting someone off is by having facial expressions or body language that is inconsistent with your words. Chris talks about this extensively in another of his books, *Unmasking the Social Engineer: The Human Element of Security* (Wiley, 2014).

You can also project and control reactions through conscious control of nonverbal signals. Recent research supports the notion that our universal "anger face" evolved as a series of facial indicators of the physical strength and ability to do harm.[15] This threat display is so instinctive in humans that even blind children make this face without ever having seen one. Researchers believe we evolved this expression to motivate effective bargaining behavior. Whatever the culture, the anger face delivers a message of power.

Even when social engineers are not engaging with targets in person, there are still ways to influence their victims' responses. Dr. Ellen Langer and fellow researchers did a fascinating study in which they had participants try to cut into a line at a copy machine.[16] They found that more people were successful at cutting if they offered a reason, even if the reason didn't make sense (for example, "Can I cut in line because I need to make copies?"). What this implies about persuasion is that providing a reason—*any* reason—while making a request increases your chance of success.

Here's one final point about psychological response: There is a whole slew of other factors that affect how a person might respond to you, but the thing to keep in mind is that for the most part, social engineers are asking for help. Helping behavior is a very large and complex topic, but some things are apparent. Most people clearly balance risk and/or the pain-in-the-butt factor when deciding whether to help. Generally speaking, people are more likely to help females and kids. People are also more likely to help when they're in good moods. Finally, people are less likely to help if there are other people around (unless someone else jumps in and helps—social proof, anyone?).

Pro tip: There are definitely things about the human condition that assist in the creation of influence. Understanding the effects of certain actions allows the social engineer to control the presentation and create a situation in which the target will give a "Yes!"

Things to Know About Manipulation

Because manipulation will undoubtedly be used against you and your organization, I wanted to do a quick overview of the most common ways you'll see it implemented. (No, I will not be providing pro tips for this section.) Figure 3-7 provides a summary of the following items:

- **Increase susceptibility:** The malicious social engineer can do all kinds of things to make people more susceptible to suggestion and bad decision-making. Earlier you read about inciting strong emotion or even simply physiological arousal as a key way to short-circuit logic centers.

- **Environmental control:** This is typically done when the malicious attacker inserts himself into the victim's social circle and asserts control. Numerous examples of this sort of activity can be found online and in real life.

- **Forced re-evaluation:** This is when the attacker makes the target doubt what he knows or has been taught. This is often done through a combination of other methods, such as threats or intimidation.

- **Removal of power:** Often used hand in hand with abuse of authority, this is when the attacker makes the victim feel as if she has no choice but to comply.

- **Punishment:** I discussed this at length in an earlier section of this chapter, but this is the direct application of a negative consequence, which results in a reaction of those who witness—rather than those who experience—the punishment.

- **Intimidation:** Whereas punishment is the application of the negative consequence, intimidation is the fear created by the threat of punishment.

Doesn't reading this stuff make you feel kind of slimy? Sure, manipulation works, but before you use it, remember you're the one who has to sleep at night.

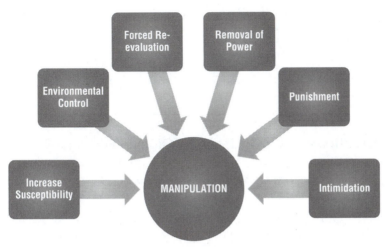

Figure 3-7: Methods of manipulation

Summary

The heart of social engineering is the conscious guiding of another's choices. Depending on your intent, your actions could be considered beneficial or malicious. At this chapter's conclusion, you now have the knowledge to

- Identify the difference between influence and manipulation

- Understand the principles of influence and why they work

- Understand that the effectiveness of influence is affected by our social nature, physiological factors, and psychological factors

- Understand basic techniques used in manipulation and be able to recognize them when they're used against you

You should now have the foundation necessary to understand phish and why they (still) work. You've gotten your basic introduction to phishing and have worked your way through primers on decision-making and influence and manipulation.

What's next? How about taking all of this information and using it to protect yourself and your organization? Chris gets into this and a lot more in Chapter 4, and he discusses a lot of our own experiences, as well as the good and bad choices made by our clients. Chapter 4 also covers both civilian and pro tips to help you protect yourself at home and at work.

Notes

1. Federal Bureau of Investigation, "Online Extortion: E-Mail Scam Includes Hit-Man Threat," FBI News Stories, January 15, 2007, http://www.fbi.gov/news/stories/2007/january/threatscam_111507.

2. Richard Gray, "Babies Not as Innocent as They Pretend," *The Telegraph* website, July 1, 2007, http://www.telegraph.co.uk/science/science-news/3298979/Babies-not-as-innocent-as-they-pretend.html.

3. Allan R. Cohen and David L. Bradford, "The Influence Model: Using Reciprocity and Exchange to Get What You Need," November 11, 2005, http://onlinelibrary.wiley.com/doi/10.1002/joe.20080/abstract, doi: 10.1002/joe.20080.

4. Chris Morran, "That Guy on the Phone Offering a Tech Support Refund Is Probably a Scammer," *The Consumerist* website, January 3, 2014, http://consumerist.com/2014/01/03/that-guy-on-the-phone-offering-a-tech-support-refund-is-probably-a-scammer/.

5. Melanie Hicken, "'Grandparent Scams' Steal Thousands from Seniors," CNN Money website, May 22, 2013, http://money.cnn.com/2013/05/22/retirement/grandparent-scams/.

6. Kathy Tomlinson, "Senior Loses $20,000 to Scammer Posing as Grandson," CBC News website, March 20, 2012, http://www.cbc.ca/news/canada/senior-loses-20-000-to-scammer-posing-as-grandson-1.1148359.

7. Andrew Wolfson, "A Hoax Most Cruel: Caller Coaxed McDonald's Managers into Strip-Searching a Worker," Courier-Journal.com, October 9, 2005, http://archive.courier-journal.com/article/20051009/NEWS01/510090392/A-hoax-most-cruel-Caller-coaxed-McDonald-s-managers-into-strip-searching-worker.

8. Mike Morris, "Police: Woman Posing as an Area Manager Steals Cash from SE Atlanta Waffle House," AJC.com, February 26,

2014, http://www.ajc.com/news/news/local/police-se-atlanta-waffle-house-robbed-by-woman-pos/ndcz4/?__federated=1.

9. Rheana Murray, "Online Dating Nightmare: Widow Robbed of $500K by Scamming Internet Companion," *Daily News* website, November 8, 2011, http://www.nydailynews.com/news/national/online-dating-nightmare-widow-robbed-500k-scamming-internet-companion-article-1.974887.

10. S. Milgram, "Behavioral Study of Obedience," *Journal of Abnormal and Social Psychology* 67(1963): 371–8.

11. Liz Phillips, "How I Got Caught Up in a 'Stranded Traveller' Phishing Scam," *The Guardian* website, November 13, 2013, http://www.theguardian.com/money/2013/nov/13/stranded-traveller-phishing-scam.

12. Matt Liebowitz, "Tips to Avoid Japanese Earthquake Phishing Scams," NBCNEWS.com, March 11, 2011, http://www.nbcnews.com/id/42036358/ns/technology_and_science-security/t/tips-avoid-japanese-earthquake-phishing-scams/#.VBYrjktg6bB.

13. Harvard Medical School, "Understanding the Stress Response," Harvard Health Publications website, March 2011, http://www.health.harvard.edu/newsletters/Harvard_Mental_Health_Letter/2011/March/understanding-the-stress-response.

14. Dan Goleman, "The Sweet Spot for Achievement," *Psychology Today* website, March 29, 2012, http://www.psychologytoday.com/blog/the-brain-and-emotional-intelligence/201203/the-sweet-spot-achievement.

15. Andrea Estrada, "The Universal 'Anger Face': Each Element Makes You Look Physically Stronger and More Formidable," *ScienceDaily* website, August 28, 2014, http://www.sciencedaily.com/releases/2014/08/140828184811.htm.

16. E. J. Langer, A. Blank, and B. Chanowitz, "The Mindlessness of Ostensibly Thoughtful Action: The Role of 'Placebic' Information in Interpersonal Interaction," *Journal of Personality and Social Psychology* 36, no. 6 (1978): 635–2.

Lessons in Protection

*"One of the major differences between school and real
life is that school first teaches you a lesson then gives you
a test; life gives you a test that teaches you a lesson."*

—Chris Hadnagy

Now that you have been thoroughly schooled by our resident shrink and phishing nerd (yes, I am talking about Michele), it is time to start applying all the knowledge you've acquired. I have talked to dozens of companies who spent hours and hours scouring the Internet for suggestions on how to educate their staffs and themselves in the art of protection. On the basis of those conversations and their frustrations, I have compiled this chapter.

What I want to do with this chapter is to break down some of the lessons that we have learned in working with some of the world's largest organizations and help you learn how to apply them. One of the things I have found is that there is a major difference between "civilian" protection tips and "pro" protection tips.

By *civilian* I mean the average, everyday person. The person who's at home without a full IT staff to call on. The one who doesn't have a resident computer nerd in the next cube who can tell you what to do as he sighs loudly at your inherent lack of technical prowess. Even a small- to medium-sized (or in some cases large) business that does not have a full-time security guru at its fingertips could fall in this category. If one of these descriptions sounds like you, pay attention to the civilian tips. The pro tips focus on suggestions that generally are appropriate for businesses that are larger and have dedicated security staff. Many of the tips apply to both civilian and pro settings; therefore, this chapter is equally important for people in both groups.

In addition, I am including a "wall of sheep" section in this chapter. If you are not familiar with that term, it comes from DEF CON, one of the world's largest hacker/security conferences. Each year at DEF CON, the folks who run the Wall of Sheep project the usernames and passwords of "sheep" who insecurely connect to networks that are not known, are unfamiliar, and are plain silly to connect to. Why? Their hope is to raise awareness about security and show people how easy it is grab these "secure" bits of data.

In this chapter, I do not list specific company names and call out dumb ideas. Instead, my wall of sheep is a list of ideas that people we've worked with have suggested and (sadly) even used that, most of the time, can lead to more harm than good.

Our goal for this chapter is to provide a resource that includes a timeless set of ideas and foundational principles to help you learn how to protect against some of the attacks covered in the first three chapters of this book.

Let's jump right in the deep end with the first lesson.

Lesson One: Critical Thinking

Category: Civilian and Pro

I feel that I would be remiss if I didn't start my first lesson off with this very crucial step—critical thinking. I discussed this in some detail in my last book, *Unmasking the Social Engineer* (Wiley, 2014), and I feel this is one of the most important tips to help people stay protected from any social-engineering attack.

Please indulge me as I reiterate the same point I made in that book. Many times people equate critical thinking with rebellion or with a lack of faith or with questioning things just for the sake of questioning them. None of those are my definition of critical thinking.

I define critical thinking as teaching yourself to not accept everything at face value. Do not accept that an e-mail is the real deal just because you are too busy to take time to evaluate it, because you are too stressed to spare a moment of thought for it, or because you have 150 other unread messages in your box. Stop for a minute and think about the e-mail. That may sound like a time-consuming task, but it doesn't take too much time to ask yourself these few questions:

- Does the e-mail come from someone I know?

- Was I expecting this e-mail?

- Are the requests being asked of me reasonable?

- Does this e-mail employ the emotional content of fear, greed, or curiosity, or, most important, does it try to get me to take an action?

Just spending two or three seconds on each of those questions can make your ability to detect phishing e-mails 100 times better.

As you read the lessons in the following sections, you can apply these questions to the lessons, and you will see how asking yourself even a couple of them can make a huge difference in detecting a real attack.

Even if you ask yourself all these questions, there are some great tips in this section to give you additional protection ideas.

How Can Attackers Bypass This Method?

Attackers don't want you to think, and they especially don't want you to think critically. They will utilize emotions that shut down your critical-thinking or logic centers (remember amygdala hijacking from Chapter 2?) and try to raise your levels of fear, sadness, or anger to get you to take an action you should not.

When you're reading an e-mail that is unexpected and from someone you don't know and it is causing you to have an emotional response, you need to beware. Step away for a few seconds and read something else before you take any action.

Lesson Two: Learn to Hover

Category: Civilian and Pro

Make believe you're sitting at home, or in the office, and you get an e-mail like the one shown in Figure 4-1. What emotions do you feel setting in?

You might first think, "I can't have my UPS packages interrupted. I better check." Or, if you don't have a UPS account, maybe fear sets in as you think, "Who set up an account in my name?"

Either way, fear or curiosity can cause you to want to click the link in the e-mail. The e-mail is branded properly, looks legit, and even looks like other UPS e-mails that you may have received in the past; all those things add weight to your belief that it's a real e-mail.

Figure 4-1: UPS phishing e-mail

But fortunately you just got done reading the first three chapters of *Phishing Dark Waters,* and you realize that this e-mail might be some form of maliciousness designed to draw you into downloading malware or giving up credentials or engaging in some other nefarious activity. What can you do first?

The link hover is what you can do. Simply move your mouse over the link, but DO NOT CLICK IT! Just let your mouse cursor hover over the link and see what happens. You should see something similar to Figure 4-2.

To help protect your account(s) from unauthorized access, we have restricted your online access, pending verification of your account

Simply click here ▼verify your account(s).

We take yo http://alexandraz.co.za/includes/MyUps/UPS.htm

If you have forgotten your password, visit **Forgot User ID or Password** on to reset it.

Thank you for choosing My UPS. To learn more

Figure 4-2: Hovering successfully *without* clicking

I'm not sure about you, but I highly doubt that UPS is storing my account info on a server in South Africa, as indicated by the .za in the domain. Because hovering revealed the URL destination and that destination is NOT UPS, this e-mail can certainly be labeled as a phish.

If you see a link like this, you need to ask yourself the critical-thinking questions:

- Does the e-mail come from someone I know?

- Was I expecting this e-mail?

- Are the requests being asked of me reasonable?

- Does this e-mail employ the emotional content of fear, greed, or curiosity, or, most important, does it try to get me to take an action?

Because the e-mail is pretty vague, you can't even answer the first question honestly. You did not expect or ask for this e-mail, and the URL goes to a completely different site. The key is to NOT click this link out of curiosity; instead, delete the e-mail straight away.

Hovering over this link, or any link, reveals where that link wants you to go. In addition, it can help you quickly answer the critical-thinking questions, making the decision clear.

Imagine that you subscribe to the monthly *Social-Engineer Newsletter.* When it comes into your e-mail box, you see a link that offers more information about social engineering—a very hot but scary topic. You first hover over the link, and you see what's shown in Figure 4-3. In some cases, a very sophisticated attacker can defeat hovering, so when you do click, double-check the URL bar to make sure you are at a legitimate address.

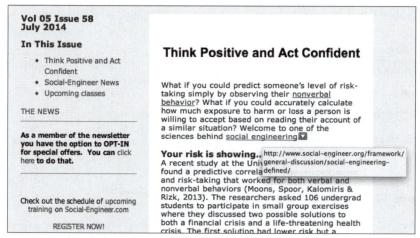

Figure 4-3: A proper and safe link to click

In the case of this e-mail, you asked for it to come to you (by subscribing to the newsletter), and the link matches the site you asked to send the letter to you. For those reasons, you can click the link.

What If I Already Clicked the Link and I Think It's Dangerous?

Unfortunately, this situation does happen, and this is a great question. First, if you are part of a company, call your IT department or security department and report the incident; this can save you and your company lots of time, headaches, and problems down the road.

But if you are not part of a company, what should you do? First, think back to what was asked of you when you clicked. Were you asked for some sort of account credentials? Were you asked to enter a username and password? Were you asked to download a file and install a "program"?

If the site asked you for an account, and you entered the credentials or you entered a new username and password, then you have to take some pretty quick and decisive action. First, you need to determine if you use that same user ID and password combo anywhere else. If you do, immediately go to those places and change your username and password. (I'm waiting. . . .)

If you do have an account with the company mentioned in the e-mail and you entered those credentials, call the company (UPS, for example) and tell it that you might have given your creds to a nefarious group. Get the company to change your credentials immediately to help make sure your account is safe.

If you installed a program as a result of the e-mail, there is a good chance you might have installed a virus, Trojan horse, or other malicious piece of software. You need to clean your computer and change most of your account usernames and passwords on another clean machine (or you can do it on your own machine right after you clean it).

Because it is impossible for me to know what type of malware you might have installed, I cannot give more detailed instructions for what you should do. Call a professional and seek some help if you don't know what to do with viruses and malware.

Either way, don't panic. Monitor your important accounts and make sure nothing "funky" is going on. Also make some changes to your passwords in those sites to give you maximum protection.

When I say not to panic, I'm not telling you that you shouldn't have a sense of urgency. By all means, you need to do these things as soon as possible, but freaking out only makes a bad situation worse. Take a deep breath, form a plan of action, and fix the things that can be fixed immediately to stop any further harm from occurring.

How Can Attackers Bypass This Method?

Attackers are aware that potential victims are being trained to hover. Many e-mail clients even look for URLs that differ from the text in the e-mail. Attackers may buy domains that closely resemble the real domain they are using in the attack. For example, if an attacker has purchased and owns the domain http://secure-YOURBANK.com, and you hover over it, you have the impression that you're seeing the "right" domain, which can cause you to trust it enough to click. This is where critical thinking plays a role; does your bank send you e-mails from this domain? When in doubt, check it out.

Other attacks can involve actually registering certificates to make the site appear legitimate and secure, but the attacker owns those certificates. Certificates can have tricky names, too, using *trusted*, *secure*, or other words that are meant to make you trust them and feel secure about clicking the links.

Attackers also work around the knowledge gained by hovering by sending e-mails from actual legitimate servers that they have compromised. They use that trust to get you to click a malicious file or link. Yes, hackers are actively compromising networks and then hiding on these networks to use mail servers or Internet-facing machines to send e-mail. Oftentimes, the attackers compromise the address books on these machines and use those addresses to contact their first set of victims.

Be very watchful and cautious. Although hovering can help keep you safe, always think before you click.

Lesson Three: URL Deciphering

Category: Civilian and Pro

Let me say up front that this section is not for webmasters or for people who know everything about the web or basic URL deciphering. It's for those people who are trying to learn enough about URLs to try to stay safe. So, if you have your hands over the keyboard so that you can type a terrible review because something in this book is too basic, please stop and skip to the next section.

Otherwise, you should continue. A URL, which is short for uniform resource locator, is basically the address of a resource on the web. It's like my address, which I would give to you so that you could enter it into your GPS to find your way right to my house. A URL is the address you type in that takes you to the resource you want. For example, in Figure 4-4 you see the URL of my corporate homepage.

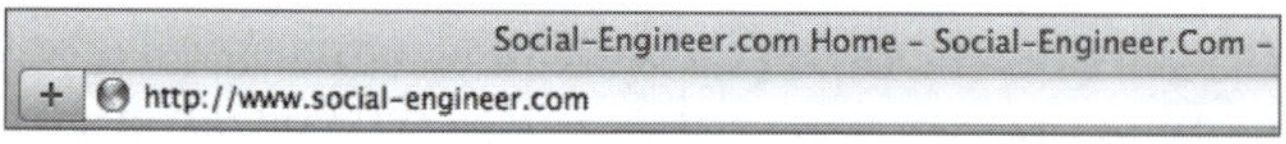

> Social-Engineer.com Home – Social-Engineer.Com –
> ✛ ⊖ http://www.social-engineer.com

Figure 4-4: The URL to my corporate homepage

There are many parts to this URL or address. You have the `http`, the `://`, the `www`, the `social-engineer`, and the `.com`, but what do each of those things mean? Let me break it down for you:

- The `http` is the protocol of the address you are visiting. `http` means a normal web address, whereas `https` indicates a web address using SSL (Secure Socket Layer) certification, and `ftp` is the protocol for an FTP server. There are many other protocols that I have not listed, but most of the time phishing e-mails use `http` or `https`.

- The `www` is the subdomain of the server. Subdomains can be things like `ww1`, `files`, `secure`, `blog`, or other such things.

- The `social-engineer` is the domain name of the server.

- The `.com` is the TLD (top-level domain) of the server. It can indicate a country, such as Russia (`.ru`), an organization (`.org`), a commercial business (`.com`), and many other indicators.

- After the TLD you may see a slash (`/`), and what comes after that can be a directory where the resource you are looking for is housed.

If I wanted to send to you a web address where there was a file called `privatefile.txt` on the normal web protocol part of the `social-engineer.com` site, it would look like Figure 4-5.

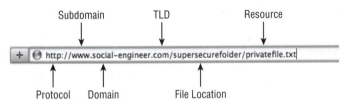

Figure 4-5: The URL to privatefile.txt

Why is this so important to understand? Because malicious phishers depend on your lack of knowledge to trick you. For example, if I am claiming I am from Microsoft and I want you to download a file called `file.txt`, can you determine based on my breakdown of the URL which of the following examples legitimately go to a Microsoft.com asset and which are a potential danger?

- `http://microsoft.com/file.txt`

- `http://secure-microsoft.com/file.txt`

- `https://secure.microsoft.com/file.txt`

- `http://microsoft.com/secure/file.txt`

- `http://rnicrosoft.com/file.txt`

How do you feel you did? Here's an explanation of each one:

- The first one is legit even though it's missing the www. It does go to a real Microsoft site.

- With the second one you have to be cautious, as secure-microsoft. com might not be owned by Microsoft.com. The "-" means it is a wholly different domain than microsoft.com.

- The third one is safe. Again, it's owned by the legit company and has the file on a secure https server. The subdomain on the legitimately owned Microsoft.com domain is "secure," unlike the second option, which tried to portray that it was secure but used a "-" instead of a "." to separate the address. The "." indicates it is part of the domain—a subdomain. Adding a "-", however, indicates a whole new domain, therefore making it untrusted.

- The fourth option is also legit. It's just in one directory down.

- The fifth one is tricky, isn't it? Look carefully. It's not m-i-c-r-o-s-o-f-t; it's r-n-i-c-r-o-s-o-f-t. But when a lowercase R and lowercase N are put close enough together in the right font, they look like a lowercase M.

These are some of the tactics that the malicious phishers use to get their victims to click links, and this is why learning to decipher URLs is so important.

Here's an important story ripped from the headlines of my life. I get paid to phish people. Yep. You read that right. And as I mentioned before, by the time you are reading this I will have been responsible for sending more than 3 million phishing e-mails this year alone. That is *a lot* of phish.

Granted, each e-mail was sent because clients asked me to help them educate their people, and I use phishing e-mails as part of promoting security awareness. I am not stealing from people, emptying their bank accounts, or ruining their lives.

Do you remember the story from Chapter 1 about the Amazon.com phish that I clicked? I mean, it was a phishing e-mail, and I've sent more than 3 million of them already—shouldn't I have known it was a phish? Yes, but I almost missed it. You know what saved me? URL deciphering, because the website the phish sent me to ended in .ru, which I knew was not a real Amazon.com address, even though the page looked identical to a real Amazon.com login page.

Even experienced security professionals can make a mistake, but good education on things like URL deciphering can save you from getting totally hacked.

How Can Attackers Bypass This Method?

Similar to the hovering method described earlier, attackers can buy domains that look legitimate. The closer one is to the real deal, the easier it is for you to believe it is real.

Attackers can also buy domains that look closely linked. Again, `secure-DOMAIN.com` is a whole new domain from `DOMAIN.com`, but if it ends in a legitimate name, a target may believe it to be real.

Also, hackers are compromising real servers all over the globe and then sending their phishing e-mails from legitimate servers. This is particularly malicious, and it can be very difficult to detect. This is where hovering and deciphering can help you not be a victim.

Critically thinking, pausing to think, and asking yourself the analytical questions can really help. Also you can keep yourself safe by being smart about reporting when you have taken an action you think you should not have.

Lesson Four: Analyzing E-mail Headers

Category: Pro

This is a pro tip because it involves getting really deep into looking into the source from which the e-mail has come. If you are not familiar with e-mail headers, then this section is not for you. Because of the plethora of e-mail clients available, I don't have space to go through how to locate the e-mail headers in every client, but I can talk about what they are and how you can use them.

You can figure out how to find e-mail headers in your client by going to the search engine of your choice and typing `Email headers in <NAME OF CLIENT>`.

Going back to my analogy of the address in your GPS, after you get to my house I can check out the history of your trip to see what route you took to get there. If you told me you took Route 1, but in fact the GPS showed you spent a lot of time on Route 2, I would know you got lost or came a different way.

E-mail headers are very similar to this, as they tell you how an e-mail got to your address. Let's take a look at one, using an e-mail I received as I wrote this chapter. The e-mail claims to be from Delta Airlines, and it's telling me my SkyMiles account needs some attention.

Let's take a look at the headers and see if we can determine whether the e-mail is real. The headers are shown in Figure 4-6.

```
☆ SkyBonus <skybonus@e.delta.com>
  To:  chris@social-engineer.com Chris
  Reply-To:  SkyBonus <support-b9f4rtybgyfvyjauze964qcgcvq1ey@e.delta.com>
  Delivered-To: chris@social-engineer.com
  Received: by 10.76.159.162 with SMTP id xd2csp204617oab; Mon, 8 Sep 2014 15:03:44 -0700 (PDT)
  Received: from mta602.e.delta.com (mta602.e.delta.com. [38.100.169.66]) by mx.google.com with ESMTP id
  s3si15952584obf.68.2014.09.08.15.03.44 for <chris@social-engineer.com>; Mon, 08 Sep 2014 15:03:44 -0700 (PDT)
  X-Received: by 10.60.93.66 with SMTP id cs2mr352647770eb.34.1410213824746; Mon, 08 Sep 2014 15:03:44 -0700
  (PDT)
  Return-Path: <bo-b9f4rtybgyfvyjauze964qcgcvq1ey@b.e.delta.com>
  Received-Spf: pass (google.com: domain of bo-b9f4rtybgyfvyjauze964qcgcvq1ey@b.e.delta.com designates
  38.100.169.66 as permitted sender) client-ip=38.100.169.66;
  Authentication-Results: mx.google.com; spf=pass (google.com: domain of bo-
  b9f4rtybgyfvyjauze964qcgcvq1ey@b.e.delta.com designates 38.100.169.66 as permitted sender) smtp.mail=bo-
  b9f4rtybgyfvyjauze964qcgcvq1ey@b.e.delta.com; dkim=pass header.i=@e.delta.com; dmarc=pass (p=QUARANTINE
  dis=NONE) header.from=e.delta.com
  Dkim-Signature: v=1; a=rsa-sha256; c=relaxed/relaxed; d=e.delta.com; s=20111007; t=1410213824; x=1425852224;
  bh=n3Bl59klfRgesEiihAa7OUfYB1N1Tbw48mWQs9A0m+x8=; h=From:Reply-To; b=na90z4QbLzz
  +WWJcC8Yr9QiKrOjAV85X+sso7j2seco90dKG4wtUNm9D/2ZLtJ9T5 KXWQPh0bJiVis3c5AOuU0hyQuNXrxMYomeQP/
  uCcyyHMuSmadyYWZQnrJS5ncqQIMK tqTxi8QDMUj4qoGXdsbLksOMqmo1TLiQGl4Z9kAA=
  Domainkey-Signature: a=rsa-sha1; q=dns; c=nofws; s=200505; d=e.delta.com;
  b=iP1n1tMBnstdGiMateWZEsGY413lJks5JM3otnDXi9n4x
  +4mtUh11VH9aXfoNeAsud5l7AGSpu8BzFvSqn3upQliXj7mGxuHS3WyZp5Ce2n+nWoToywylz+Qyz+dDZfq6H
  +4lXvridsL60VkWSGTXkV6jDnSWNh6tZBKTcwBwYM=; h=Date:Message-ID:List-Unsubscribe:From:To:Subject:MIME-
  Version:Reply-To:Content-type;
  Message-Id: <b9f4rtybgyfvyjauze964qcgcvq1ey.14705548104.3047@mta602.e.delta.com>
  List-Unsubscribe: <mailto:rm-0b9f4rtybgyfvyjauze964qcgcvq1ey@e.delta.com>
  Mime-Version: 1.0
  Content-Type: multipart/alternative; boundary="=b9f4rtybgyfvyjauze964qcgcvq1ey"
  Important Information Regarding your Account
```

Figure 4-6: Good or bad headers?

Well, if you are like me, you think that Figure 4-6 looks really confusing. Table 4-1 breaks it down in parts in a cleaner form so that you can see it clearly.

Table 4-1: Breakdown of the Delta.com E-mail Header

HEADERNAME	HEADERVALUE
To	chris@social-engineer.com Chris <chris@social-engineer.com>
Reply-To	SkyBonus <support-b9f4rtybgyfvyjauze964qcgcvq1ey@e.delta.com>
Delivered-To	chris@social-engineer.com
X-Received	by 10.60.93.66 with SMTP id cs2mr3526 47770eb.34.1410213824746; Mon, 08 Sep 2014 15:03:44 -0700 (PDT)

Return-Path	<bo-b9f4rtybgyfvyjauze964qcgcvq1ey@b.e. delta.com>
Received-Spf	pass (google.com: domain of bo-b9f4rtybgyfvyjauze964qcgcv q1ey@b.e.delta.com designates 38.100.169.66 as permitted sender) client-ip=38.100.169.66;
Authentication- Results	mx.google.com; spf=pass (google.com: domain of bo-b9f4rtybgyfvyjauze964 qcgcvq1ey@b.e.delta.com designates 38.100.169.66 as permitted sender) smtp.mail=bo-b9f4rtybgyfvyjauze964 qcgcvq1ey@b.e.delta.com; dkim=pass header.i=@e.delta.com; dmarc=pass (p=QUARANTINE dis=NONE) header.from=e. delta.com
Dkim-Signature	v=1; a=rsa-sha256; c=relaxed/ relaxed; d=e.delta.com; s=20111007; t=1410213824; x=1425852224; bh=n3 Bl59kfRgesEiihAa7OUfYB1N1Tbw48mW Qs9A0m+x8=; h=From:Reply-To; b=n a90z4QbLzz+WWJcC8Yr9QiKrOjAV85X+ sso7j2seco90dKG4wtUNm9D/2ZLtJ9T5 KXWQPh0bJiVis3c5AOuU0hyQuNXrxMYomeQP/ uCcyyHMuSmadyYWZQnrJS5ncqQlMK tqTxi8QDMUj4qoGXdsbLksOMqmo1TLiQGl4Z9kAA=
Domainkey- Signature	a=rsa-sha1; q=dns; c=nofws; s=200505; d=e.delta.com; b=iP1n1tMBnstdGiMateWZE sGY413IJks5JM3otnDXi9n4x+4mtUh11VH9aXf oNeAsud5l7AGSpu8BzFvSqn3upQliXj7mGxuHS 3WyZp5Ce2n+nWoToywylz+Qyz+dDZfq6H+41Xv ridsL60VkWSGTXkV6jDnSWNh6tZBKTcwBwYM=; h=Date:Message-ID:List- Unsubscribe:From:To:Subject:MIME- Version:Reply-To:Content-type;
Message-Id	<b9f4rtybgyfvyjauze964qc- gcvq1ey.14705548104.3047@ mta602.e.delta.com>
List- Unsubscribe	<mailto:rm- 0b9f4rtybgyfvyjauze964qcgcvq1ey@e. delta.com>
Mime-Version	1.0
Content-Type	multipart/alternative; boundary="=b9f4r tybgyfvyjauze964qcgcvq1ey"

We can see the e-mail was sent to the right address, and both the `Reply-To` and the `Return-Path` are clearly going to `delta.com` addresses. We can also see `delta.com` in both the `Domainkey-Signature` and the `Message-Id` portions. All of these things point to it being a legitimate e-mail from the source it claims, which means it can be trusted to be real.

At the same time I received the Delta.com e-mail, though, the e-mail shown in Figure 4-7 arrived. It promised me a great deal on health insurance.

Figure 4-7: Health care savings for me?

Hovering alone can save me from this one, but let's take a look at the headers, which are shown in Figure 4-8.

What can you pick out even without a nice clean table? Do you see the domain that was promised in the e-mail (`usinsuranceonline.com`)? Nope. Instead this header is littered with `frenbury.eu`. Kinda weird that a non-U.S. site is offering me savings on U.S. insurance, right? Take a look at the breakdown of the headers in Table 4-2.

```
☆ USInsurance <USInsurance@frenbury.eu>
  To: logan@social-engineer.org Chris
  Delivered-To: logan@social-engineer.org
  Received: by 10.42.215.69 with SMTP id hd5csp584155icb; Thu, 11 Sep 2014 11:19:04 -0700 (PDT)
  Received: from 1d2e4wpsq.frenbury.eu (1d2e4wpsq.frenbury.eu. [74.199.201.16]) by mx.google.com with ESMTP id
  a93si2170300qge.120.2014.09.11.11.19.04 for <logan@social-engineer.org>; Thu, 11 Sep 2014 11:19:04 -0700 (PDT)
  Received: by 03510818.1d2e4wpsq.frenbury.eu (amavisd-new, port 10820) with ESMTP id 03XWWIA5108QVVLY18; for
  <logan@social-engineer.org>; Thu, 11 Sep 2014 11:19:05 -0700
  X-Received: by 10.140.90.42 with SMTP id w39mr3951809qgd.88.1410459544779; Thu, 11 Sep 2014 11:19:04 -0700
  (PDT)
  Return-Path: <USInsurance@frenbury.eu>
  Received-Spf: pass (google.com: domain of USInsurance@frenbury.eu designates 74.199.201.16 as permitted sender)
  client-ip=74.199.201.16;
  Authentication-Results: mx.google.com; spf=pass (google.com: domain of USInsurance@frenbury.eu designates
  74.199.201.16 as permitted sender) smtp.mail=USInsurance@frenbury.eu
  Content-Transfer-Encoding: 8bit
  Content-Language: en-us
  Mime-Version: 1.0
  Message-Id: <5820885563631658201301255298835@1d2e4wpsq.frenbury.eu>
  Content-Type: text/html; charset="UTF-8"
  Health Insurance, no longer breaks the bank I Get no cost-oblig quotes from all the top companies here
```

Figure 4-8: Headers part II

Table 4-2: Breakdown of the USInsurance E-mail Header

HEADERNAME	HEADERVALUE
To	logan@social-engineer.org Chris <logan@ social-engineer.org>
Delivered-To	logan@social-engineer.org
X-Received	by 10.140.90.42 with SMTP id w39mr395 1809qgd.88.1410459544779; Thu, 11 Sep 2014 11:19:04 -0700 (PDT)
Return-Path	<USInsurance@frenbury.eu>
Received-Spf	pass (google.com: domain of USInsurance@frenbury.eu designates 74.199.201.16 as permitted sender) client-ip=74.199.201.16;
Authentication-Results	mx.google.com; spf=pass (google.com: domain of USInsurance@frenbury.eu designates 74.199.201.16 as permitted sender) smtp.mail=USInsurance@frenbury.eu
Content-Transfer-Encoding	8bit
Content-Language	en-us
Mime-Version	1.0
Message-Id	<5820885563631658201301255298835@1d2e4w-psq.frenbury.eu>
Content-Type	text/html; charset="UTF-8"

It is pretty clear that the domain from the header has nothing to do with the domain given in the e-mail. The return path and authentication results have nothing to do with USInsurance; instead they're from a European site. A security-minded person would take this as a red flag if it is an untrusted and unknown source, would report this e-mail, would not click the link, and would delete the message.

How Can Attackers Bypass This Method?

Is examining the header a surefire way of staying protected? No. As we speak, there are phishing e-mails hitting networks with one purpose in mind: to infiltrate their networks and gain access to a machine to use as an SMTP server. Why?

Raise your hand if you ever received an e-mail from a friend only to find out later that it was not legitimate. (How many of you are actually sitting in front of a book with your hands up?)

As Michele mentioned in Chapter 3, our friends can easily influence us. Phishers know this, and they also know that there's no better way to get you to trust an attachment, link, or file than by making you think that it comes from someone you already trust.

Phishers will gain access to legitimate computers and then use them as outbound mail servers to send malicious e-mails to all the contacts, friends, and other random addresses in the inbox. If you got one of those types of e-mails and you analyzed the headers, what would you see?

A legitimate e-mail is what you would see. If you choose to try to analyze headers, it is important to still ask yourself the critical-thinking questions before you trust any e-mail. Although analyzing the e-mail headers can save you from clicking a fraudulent e-mail, it is not a 100 percent guarantee that you'll catch every fraudulent message.

Lesson Five: Sandboxing

Category: Pro

First, I want to talk about what sandboxing is, which will help you understand why it is a pro-related tip. *Sandboxing* is a term used in the tech field to describe creating an environment where one can run untested or untrusted code. That code may contain viruses or malware, or it might be untrusted for other reasons. So before users want it to run on their main system or network, they have an environment that enables them to execute the code with little effect on the host or main environment. The concept, very simplified, is diagrammed in Figure 4-9.

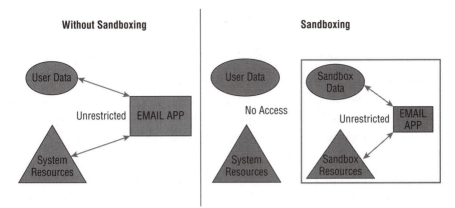

Figure 4-9: Sandboxing simplified

The theory is good, and it works for many threats. I have actually worked with companies that sandbox all incoming e-mail. Links are verified with automated systems, and attachments are scanned and even opened. They're passed through only if they are deemed safe and friendly.

The concept of a sandbox is quite smart, but it's also quite advanced. (That said, there are apps being sold for iOS and Android devices that offer sandboxes for e-mail on those devices so attachments can be opened in an environment that will not affect the host.) In general, it is not something that many average home users or small-business owners who are not that tech savvy can imagine implementing.

Many large companies use virtual machines to create sandboxes. This environment allows for a "virtual" computer of any operating system to be run, so e-mail or other applications can be tested to determine whether they are safe.

Although I won't go into *how* to set up a sandbox (because that's not the purpose of this book), I wanted to mention it as an alternative idea for keeping your people safe from phishing attacks.

How Can Attackers Bypass This Method?

As I write this chapter, I was reading a story about a particular version of malware attached to phishing e-mails from a group called Quarian. It was known in 2011 for crafting attachments that looked like PDF, DOC, or XLS files but were actually maliciously encoded files that contained malware. The group specialized in spear phish targeting government agencies.

Now, it appears, Quarian is back but with an even more evil upgrade. The new version contains some features to be noted:

- It installs itself as a Windows service, not just a program in RUN.
- It runs a series of commands that connect to a foreign server to download its payload.
- It relies on an AppID or a command-line interaction, and consequently *it will not be detected in a sandbox environment.*

In addition, more than six years ago when I worked with Mati Aharoni, security professional and creator of BackTrack (now Kali Linux), he showed me a piece of malware that had the ability to tunnel through a virtual machine's connection directly to the host.

What does all this mean? Attackers are getting smarter, and they are learning ways to bypass the methods that we are coming up with to bypass their attacks. (Say that five times fast.)

I say the rule with any technological solution to a human-based problem is, "Technology alone cannot keep you safe from the social engineer."

Along with many of the good ideas we've seen and come up with, Michele and I have encountered some pretty awful ideas along the way. The next section discusses those ideas and why they may not be so great.

The "Wall of Sheep," or a Net of Bad Ideas

We have heard some concepts that, on the surface, sound like they would be great ways to help employees stay safe. Some of them might even have had a glimmer of hope for being successful, but we are classifying them under the topic of "Bad Ideas."

The following are suggestions that we have actually been told were in use at companies, and we discuss what they are and why they are potentially bad ideas.

Copy and Paste Your Troubles Away

One suggestion that I actually saw written in one company's training went something like this: "If you are unsure whether a link you received in an e-mail is safe to click, highlight the link, copy it, and then paste it into the URL section of the browser."

I am sure all of you can immediately see why this goes on the top of the list as one of the worst ideas in history. But, just in case, let's analyze it. If you receive a phishing e-mail with a link to `www.superbadhackingsitethatwillruinyourlife.com`, and you highlight it, copy it, and paste it, where do you go? Yes, you guessed it; you still go to `www.superbadhackingsitethatwillruinyourlife.com`.

"But," you say, "what if the URL reads something like `www.micro-soft.com` and the back-end URL is the bad one, then won't copy and paste work?"

OK, technically, if you can get your users to copy just that text, they go to the copied link. But if the users mistakenly click the link instead of copying it, if they mistakenly right-click and then choose Copy Link instead of just copying, or if they do any combination of these things, they still end up at the malicious site and potentially load malware on your network.

So, to be safe, we tell the average user not to click the link. Do not go near it. Do not copy and paste it. And, unless you are familiar with how to decipher URLs, do not attempt to analyze it.

Sharing Is Caring

Another idea goes something like this: "Oh, I just got this e-mail that I think may be a phish. Let me just click Forward and send it to my five most techie friends so they can tell me if it's bad."

If you do this, all you've done is forward a potentially dangerous and malicious e-mail to five of your friends. If those friends work for the same company, you may have furthered the potential damage in the company. And if they work in other companies, you may be spreading the virus, essentially doing the social engineer's job for him.

It is almost like saying, "I think I have the flu. I am going to go cough on five of my best friends, and if they get sick they can tell me what it was."

In one audit I did that involved a USB key drop, we loaded a USB key with a PDF file that was encoded with a piece of code that just "phoned home." After it hit our server, it was programmed to tie into a Metasploit server and give us a "shell" (or connection back to a user's computer) remotely. The PDF inside was labeled `EmployeeBonuses.PDF`.

We dropped the USB in the location agreed upon and then headed back to the office. By the time we got back, we already had seven shells. We knew we dropped only one device. We started to look at what units the shells were on, and we found them in HR, IT, and a few others in those same departments.

Were we confused? Yes, but we were also happy, as we had many compromised systems to choose from. Later on, we asked what happened, and we were told that when the first person tried to open the `EmployeeBonuses.PDF` file and it crashed, he took it to a buddy in HR who was more tech savvy. When the file crashed on the second person's computer, they took it to an IT buddy, who in turn tried it on all three of his machines. Finally, the HR guy, frustrated, just went up to a random employee and said, "Try to open this," and she did.

In essence, these people were sneezing all over the company as they tried to see their bonuses. In this case, sharing is *not* caring, despite what your grandma might have told you. The same goes with suspected phish. Hopefully, your company has a designated method for reporting phishing e-mails. If it doesn't, call me as soon as you can.

My Mobile Is Secure

I have actually overheard someone telling another person, "If you think it's a malicious e-mail, just open it up on your <iPad/iPhone/Android device/Windows mobile device/insert other device type here>. They can't get viruses like your laptop."

After I got done with the inevitable face palm, I politely explained to the person that there is a plethora of mobile-based malware and viruses out there today. I explained the misconception, how dangerous it was, and why it was still a huge threat.

Now let's take this a step further. Imagine your company allows BYOD (bring your own device), and one of your users is sending all his spam to his iPad so he can open it on what he considers his personal sandbox. Now he brings that device to your office, and it's dripping with every flavor of web infection known to man. What does he do then? Connects it to your corporate network, of course.

Your corporate network now becomes the tissue on which every user's virus is wiped. The open-it-on-your-mobile-device idea is one piece of 'advice' you want to squash right away.

A Good Antivirus Program Will Save You

Antivirus: The name itself should tell you something. It is trying to stop *viruses*. How does it do that? Well, viruses have signatures—that is, inside of the virus there is a set of code that fingerprints it. Just like your fingerprint identifies you, a virus's fingerprint identifies it.

These fingerprints are put into the databases of antivirus software, and then your computer is scanned. If the software finds a website, file, folder, or program with one of these signatures, it eradicates that asset so no more damage can be done.

Awesome, no? Yes, it is. But let's face it, antivirus (AV) software is a management tool, not a security tool. AVs save you from viruses with *known* signatures. But what if the virus is brand new and not finger-printed yet? What if the virus is using polymorphic shellcode (shellcode that changes its signature every time it loads)?

You think me daft? Am I dabbling in the stuff of sci-fi? No, siree. My good friend David Kennedy, who is the creator of a tool used by penetra-tion testers called The Social Engineer Toolkit, does exactly that. One of his attacks in the tool uses the very same shellcode, and, most of the time, it's undetected by all AVs. If one of the good guys can do it, we can assume the bad guys are doing it, too.

Does this mean you should ditch the AV and stop wasting money? No, absolutely not. Keep the AV because it catches those pesky viruses that have been around a while, but don't rely on it as a foolproof savior, because the AV isn't going to save you from an attacker with intent.

Summary

Speaking of shellcode in the last section makes me think of an encoder— a little program that one can use to encode shellcode to give it a new signature—called Shikata Ga Nai. It is a polymorphic encoder, and the name is Japanese for "Nothing can be done," or as we roughly translated it, "There is no hope." After reviewing information like what's discussed in the preceding section, you might feel all shikata ga nai, but don't worry. It's my aim to give you back some hope.

Let's list what we know so far:

- The bad guys are advanced, determined, and driven. They seem to be ahead of you and rely on your weaknesses to win.

- Technology alone cannot save you, and it should not be viewed as a fix for social engineering.

- Phishing is a real threat, one that can make you lose your bank account or nation's secrets and everything in between.

- If it is your job to keep your company safe, you need to find those people who are giving you bad advice and eradicate them . . . I mean, eradicate the bad advice, not the person.

If all of this is true, then what can you do?

Education is the key to the solution. You have to work with your company to get consistent, timely, real-world education that sticks with the user to change the mind set and create a security-minded culture.

Right now you might be saying, "But I sat all my people through 30 or even 60 minutes of CBTs, I gave them lengthy tests, and I send them five-page e-mails about this topic every month, and they just aren't getting it. So, education doesn't work!"

I agree with you. That type of education does not work. How many e-mails do you get a day? 50, 100, 200? Do you also have a real job that you must attend to? Now pile on meetings, calls, reports, personal e-mails, personal problems, work stress, and a 60-minute CBT that is mandatory. What do you think most people are doing with that training?

I can tell you, but you don't want to hear it, as it will just be the sound of money burning in the fireplace.

The answer to this problem is not as bad as you think, and it doesn't involve reprogramming all your users, firing everyone, and starting over or going back to paper and pen.

And it is the sole topic of Chapter 5.

Plan Your Phishing Trip: Creating the Enterprise Phishing Program

"Do or do not . . . there is no try."

—Yoda in *Star Wars Episode V: The Empire Strikes Back*

Let's say you read the first four chapters and are saying, "Yep, I get it, and I 100 percent agree . . . now what?"

Believe it or not, I meet people like you every day. Companies who see what is happening in the world around us and realize there is a need for security. They understand that phishing, vishing, and social engineering are used in almost every attack, and they don't want to be the next statistic in the newspaper.

Many security professionals start with a quick Google search to find which vectors are being used the most. It doesn't take long to see that phishing is almost always at the top of the list. The next logical progression is to start searching for phishing education help.

One company might tell you, "Just use our templates and you will be amazed." Another might say, "You must go super hard-core on your employees to scare them into shape." Yet another might propose this wisdom: "If you embarrass and humiliate them, they will learn." And a fourth company might suggest, "A balance between education and healthy fear is the best."

How do you decide what to do? How do you decide what program can help you the best?

As mentioned in Chapter 4, Michele and I have sent—are you ready for this?—more than 3 million phishing e-mails in just the past year. With that many phishing e-mails under our belts, we have collected the best, the worst, and the plain ol' stupid as far as ideas go.

The purpose of this chapter is to outline what we have used to help our clients reduce the click ratio on phish from an average of over 80 percent to an average of 5 percent in just a couple years. The content for this chapter was developed over the course of the last few years; it has been tried and tested, and now we present it here for you.

NOTE *Click ratio* is the ratio that represents how many employees actually click on phishing e-mails.

But here's the rub: I am a vendor of corporate phishing protection programs. So how do I give you all this knowledge and teach you how to protect yourself and/or your company without making it sound like a giant sales pitch? *That* is a topic that Michele and I labored over for many a moon, and we've come up with a good approach.

It has taken us years to develop and test this process. Now we have refined the process enough that it is imperative to get it into your hands as soon as possible so that we can help as many people as possible to be prepared to battle the phish market.

NOTE I once went to do some work in China, and I was told to go visit the giant markets where vendors peddle their wares. One piece of advice stuck with me: I was told that there would be dozens of people trying to get me to buy their wares, and all I had to do was to simply say, "Boo hao" (pronounced "boo how"), which means, basically, "No good." As a result of my refusal, the vendors would lower the price as I walked away. This simple two-word sentence saved me hundreds of dollars at these markets.

The goal for this chapter is to teach you the little things I have learned over the last few years so that your time in the "market" is much easier and more profitable.

First we go over some basics, then we start to develop the program together, and finally we walk through a method for implementing the program in a company—regardless of whether that company includes 100 people or 100,000 people.

The Basic Recipe

Most people who know me know I love to cook (and to eat), and any great meal starts with some very basic questions:

- What do I want to eat?
- What recipes should I use?
- What is the purpose of the meal?
- Are there other aspects to the meal I need to prepare, such as plating, sides, and so on?

Ask Michele these questions for me, and the answer she will tell you is simply "lamb"—but I should get back on topic because this chapter isn't actually about food. It's about our phishing program. But a phishing program is similar to a meal, and you must start with a few basic questions before you can even start the development of the program.

NOTE Don't be fooled—phishing your organization sounds simple, but just jumping in and sending phishing e-mails without answering the questions in the following sections will lead to disaster.

Why?

Asking "Why?" seems simple enough, but how you answer is something that can really change the face of your phishing program. Why are you starting a program? Are you running a phishing simulation for any of the following reasons?

You Need to Comply with Regulations

Corporate policy, the board, or, in some cases, contract negotiations can dictate how they want your organization to be tested. We have run into this reason when we've worked on some large contracts. Government regulations or other such matters require the company to run a few phishing simulations and report the results.

Compliance is not a bad reason to start a phishing program, but when it is the only motivation, more often than not we have observed that companies do the bare minimum to get the numbers they need. Compliance-motivated testing can lead to using weaker templates and looking only at click ratios.

Again, it's good to determine a baseline, but it is important to not make compliance the only motivation for a phishing program.

You Are Told to Run a Phishing Simulation

Sometimes a boss, the CISO, or some other person tells a department to organize and send a phishing simulation. When I hear that this reason is the motivation for starting a program, I generally ask to speak to the requestor so I can find out what reasons (of those listed here) that person has for being motivated to do the simulation. As the person being told to start the program, you should ask these questions of the requestor, too.

You're Trying to Increase Security Awareness

Many companies include a phishing simulation as part of their annual program to continually test the population for susceptibility to phishing e-mails. These tests can be organized and sent once per month or one per quarter, and they almost always lead to education.

Security awareness is a very common reason to start a phishing simulation, and it's the sign of a very forward-thinking company. Regularly engaging in phishing simulations has a dramatic effect on the security culture of a population, and that is great news.

In addition, we have personally seen people go from not even knowing what phish are to being able to pick them out even at the most difficult level (both at work and at home). This reason for starting is powerful and can have long-term effects on how your people value security awareness and how they view how much their company cares for them and their welfare.

You've Recently Experienced a Security Event

Many companies run phishing simulations after a breach or similar security event. The goal is to first set a baseline, educate people or fix some of the problems, and then retest to see if there is an adjustment.

Of course, it is sad to see that companies at times wait until they have been breached to wake up and smell the phish, but at least they are doing something. I have seen phishing simulations used to report to the board the state of the population, which then leads to including ongoing phishing in security awareness. This is positive, of course, and can lead to the population getting the education it needs to remain secure.

My opinion is that organizations should not wait to be breached to start a program. The "ostrich" method of security (sticking your head in the sand and assuming you will never be breached) rarely works. The security community has stopped saying, "If you get breached," and has started saying, "When you get breached," because it seems that sooner or later we all will be breached.

Don't be the low-hanging fruit; train and educate before phishers pick you off the tree.

You're Doing It as Part of a Penetration Test

It is becoming more common for companies to include phishing vectors as part of a penetration test (pentest). This can be done in multiple ways. In one method the phish leads to a shell (or remote access to your network) as the phish is loaded with executable files or attachments that contain code to allow the pentester to connect to the network remotely. In another method the phish leads to a page that harvests credentials. With a third method the destination of the phish is a 404 Error Page, and the employee is never alerted that he or she is part of a phishing simulation. The phish in a fourth option leads to an education page.

Whatever choice your company makes, it is a good idea to start including phishing as part of the annual pentest. I know that statement opens up another huge set of questions. For example, is my pentest company able to phish well? Does it have experience in this area of security? How realistic should we be with the test?

All of these are great questions, and you should have clear answers in your head before you speak to the pentest company to make sure you get the services you want and need.

Why Ask Why?

Okay, so you now have a clear picture of some basic reasons why you might want to start a program, but *why* is it important to know why you want to start phishing?

It's simple. The answer affects the way the program is structured, the phish you use, the vendor you choose, and the results you can rightfully expect.

For example, imagine your reason for starting is a breach. You can't expect any phishing vendor to help you go instantaneously from a

90 percent click ratio down to 10 percent, right? Immediately after a breach is a scary time that is full of quick movements and quick decisions. The main objectives are to get people educated about what phishing is, what it looks like, and how to mitigate rather than to lower your overall ratios.

However, if your reason is security awareness over the next 12 months, you can rightfully expect to see drastic changes.

Knowing why you want to run a phishing program before you start "cooking" helps you perfect the phishing meal to be more palatable to both your population and your higher-ups.

After you know why you want to run a phishing program, the next piece is to determine how you plate it.

What's the Theme?

When preparing a meal you probably think about the theme. For example, if you were planning a table setting for a Super Bowl party, you probably wouldn't use the same theme as you would for a 20th anniversary dinner for your spouse, right? (Well, I certainly hope you wouldn't just throw some wings on a napkin and sit in front of the tube if you were celebrating your 20th anniversary.) The point is that the theme of the meal changes the way it is presented.

This might sound similar to the questions in the preceding section, but there are some major differences. The following sections cover some common themes.

Generic

This category covers anything from the ancient 419 scams to the Viagra ads. I will say that I don't see these types of phish used much anymore, but if your organization has never phished before and you want to start the program off with some e-mail that are easier to spot as phish in order to warm up the population, you can consider this an appetizer.

Generic phish can help set a baseline for you to see how your people respond to anything with a link and to find out whether they are taking the proper actions when they spot something suspicious.

One caution: If you decide to work with a vendor or if you are starting off on your own, make sure that your program does not stay in this generic section for too long. It gets frustrating for the users if they are good at spotting phish to be tested with something easy for an extended period of time.

Media/News

We have seen a lot more of this type of phish in the wild recently. Here are some examples:

- "Someone has run a background check on you."
- "Breaking news. A bomb has gone off in *<insert location here>*."
- "*<Insert disaster here>* Major news! Click here to find out more."
- "You are being requested for an interview on CNN. Please pick a time slot that works for you."

Whatever the reason, news and media are used widely in phishing e-mails, and this theme can draw a lot of interest from your population. It can also help to educate your users on how to identify real versus fake news stories and what a phisher may be looking for when using this particular theme.

Other External Topics/Sources

The external type of e-mails I listed in the first two sections are just samples. There are literally dozens, if not hundreds, more that can be included in this list.

Because I can't list them all here, I will include any other theme that comes from an external source that's not linked to your business by either internal sources or vendors. Phishing e-mails that appear to be from Facebook, Amazon.com, and LinkedIn all can go in this list.

Vendors

One technique social engineers use when looking at target companies is discovering all vendors their targets use. Phishers research waste management companies, phone and Internet providers, electric companies, software and hardware vendors, and even your security service providers.

Why would this information be so valuable to them? It's because social engineers know that you and your staff are more likely to trust and click a link, open attachments, or provide information if it comes from a trusted vendor rather than a new one.

Phishers bank on this fact and want to get you to "take an action that is not in your best interest," and they're willing to use your vendors' names to make it happen. A social engineer who knows that your waste management company is called Waste-R-Us and has a website at www.wasterus.com knows that it might just work to send you an e-mail from accounting@waterus.com (yes, that's misspelled on purpose) to get you to open a PDF with maliciously embedded code inside.

Here's the conundrum: Is it legal, ethical, or moral for a security provider to use the logos and branding of vendors to test the population? I have some thoughts on this, which I discuss in "The Big, Fat, Not-So-Legal Section" below.

Internal

E-mails that look like they're from an internal source are a great theme to help your population learn the dangers of phishing. Having URLs that look similar to your corporate URL or using e-mails that purport to be from the HR, IT, or admin departments or from C-level managers can help your population to see that phishers will do this all the time. It's a good method to help your staff become skilled with URL deciphering and reading e-mail addresses more closely. (Read Chapter 4 for more information on these protection methods.)

How far do you go with this? Our company never recommends starting with the highest level up front. You don't want to leave your population feeling hopeless. We suggest when you get to this theme that you start off mild, leaving other indicators in the e-mail, and then work up to the hardest level.

Yes, I hear the argument some of you are making: "The bad guys don't care and will use the highest level today." I agree with that, but don't forget the simple fact that *we* are not the bad guys. My intent and goals are different. My goal when I work with a company is not to show you how "stupid your users are" but to help build a quality educational program that makes your population more secure at work and at home. That outcome is rarely achieved by making people feel stupid and hopeless. So, although starting easy is not 100 percent realistic, it is the method that works.

By now you can get the sense that the theme is just as important as the reasons why you're starting a phishing program. It is vital that you take the time to really carefully think about these two sections before you move to the next. Have a clear picture why you want to start a phishing program and the types of themes you are comfortable starting off with and then you can determine what features of a phishing program might help make it more realistic, educational, and successful.

The Big, Fat, Not-So-Legal Section

Before I continue with our regularly scheduled program, I need to pause to discuss this topic that is always a hot one for debate in the phishing community: "To logo or not to logo; that is the question."

Imagine you get a phishing e-mail from some group in Greece, and it looks just like a UPS e-mail—complete with logo, official wording, and even legalese in the footer. Although the e-mail is designed to look like it comes from UPS, the links all go to a malicious credential-harvesting site intended to steal passwords, usernames, account data, and more.

With evildoers using this technique more and more an increasing number of companies are opting to use trademarks in phishing simulations to test their employees' reactions to these e-mails. This decision has sparked some serious debate among phishing professionals, vendors, legal departments, and, of course, the companies who have had their logos used.

Before I say anything else, let me start by saying this: *I am not a lawyer, and this is not legal advice.* You should consult an attorney before you make any decisions about whether to use logos or other branding in your phishing simulations. Now, with that out of the way, here's some basic information.

Trademarks are the words, images, phrases, and symbols used by companies to indicate that their products or services belong to them. The main federal law governing trademarks in the United States is the Lanham Act, 15 U.S.C. §§ 1111–1129. Although trademark law has developed over decades and has many complex wrinkles, it's safe to say there are a few basic requirements that a plaintiff must establish before a court will find that someone has infringed on a trademark or used the mark in an unauthorized way:

- The plaintiff has to prove that it has a valid mark.
- The plaintiff must show the defendant used the same or a similar mark in commerce in connection with the sale or advertising of goods or services without the plaintiff's consent.
- The plaintiff must show that the defendant's use of the mark is likely to cause confusion.

The second item in the preceding list is key for phishing purposes. This suggests it would be safer not to use logos in phishing e-mail simulations to advertise or propose the sale of any product, even if you're just doing it to dupe your clients or your own employees.

There are some other considerations to think about before you decide whether to use a trademark in a phishing e-mail:

- Could you or your client possibly ask the mark holder's permission to use the logo or other branding in a phishing exercise before you use it? (If so, make sure to get the permission in writing.)

- Even if you have a good argument that you aren't infringing on anyone's trademark and might eventually win that case in court, lawsuits are expensive, time-consuming, and stressful. If a company did decide to sue you, are you prepared to spend the time, money, and energy to defend the case in court?

- Does your client use the vendor you are considering using so the phishing e-mail is realistic? If not, is it really worth it? Let's say I saw a brand-new UPS phishing e-mail that is working on everyone, but my present client uses only FedEx. Wouldn't it be silly to suggest using the UPS logo in a phishing e-mail to the client's employees just for the sake of using it?

The answers to these questions can make a huge difference in the way you think about how and whether to use trademarks in phishing simulations.

Now, just because I know you might be asking what I think about this matter, I will tell you my opinion. I am all for the use of trademarks. Let me illustrate why with a cooking reference. The first time I tried to make a cheesecake I didn't have a springform pan. The cheesecake was okay, but it was not as authentic as the real deal. Those of you who make cheesecake know that you don't just go and buy a springform pan and start using it. It takes some practice and prep, but after you've done those things, you have an amazing finished product.

A branded phishing e-mail simulation is a very advanced technique that takes some practice to perfect. If you partner with a vendor, make sure to ask its practices on using vendor logos, and if you are preparing a program on your own, make sure you have answered the questions I posed earlier in this section.

The last thing I will say about this before moving back to our regularly scheduled chapter is that I have had using logos go great many times and go bad a couple times. When I say bad, I don't mean that I got sued, but I did have some folks who were not too happy with me.

Now, let's say you want to use branding but you are a little nervous about going all the way at first; what can you do? Take a look at Figure 5-1; what do you see?

Figure 5-1: UPS or USP logo?

If you used this logo in a phishing simulation, would it be enough to give your e-mail the proper look to test the employees? Can you do it without getting in any trouble?

Well, I can't answer these questions for you or your organization, so talk to your legal department, explain the issue, and see how it feels about this type of phishing simulation. Think about whether your company or vendor might be able to get the trademark owner's sign-off. Consult with your lawyers and ask them to help you figure out how to stay on the right side of the law—because the bad guys are using branding, it works, and users need to be educated about the methods the bad guys use.

Developing the Program

By now you understand why you are phishing your population. You have a clearly defined theme for your program. You even have a clear sense whether you want to brand or not.

The nagging question that remains is, "How do I even start?" Michele and I developed a program that we have seen work in a lot of companies from so many varying industries that we felt it was vital to share it.

Yes, as I write this I am presently helping more than a couple handfuls of clients run their programs for them, but I still felt it was direly important to share this knowledge with the masses.

The program really is quite simple, even though it will sound complicated at times. But the principle behind it is the same as it is for anything that's worth doing. You don't start a workout program by lifting the heaviest weights on earth, right? You start small, build up, and continue to break down, maintain, grow, then break down, maintain, and grow. This phishing program is not much different than that. We will help you break down, teach you how to maintain that level, and then explain how you grow. Then you repeat the cycle.

Before you know it, you will be an Olympic-style phishing expert. This program can be broken down into six sections:

- Setting a baseline
- Setting the difficulty level
- Writing the phish
- Tracking and statistics
- Reporting
- Repeating

The following sections break down each step.

Setting a Baseline

I had this wonderful opportunity to run a fun version of the polygraph at the popular security conference DerbyCon. We got to ask people really embarrassing questions to see if they would tell the truth or try to lie and get away with it. The polygraph examiner would first set a baseline—that is, the examiner would ask a question there is no reason to lie about in order to see the person's normal response. For us that question was, "Are the lights on in this room?"

This baseline would help the examiner to see where the person's heart rate, breathing rate, and sweat production normally was when the person was being honest. Then as the test went on, fluctuations could be gauged against that baseline.

A phishing program that is successful starts with this same philosophy—a baseline. But how do you set a baseline for a phishing program? There are two philosophies: the "warned baseline" and the "surprise phish baseline."

The Warned Baseline

The first idea for setting a baseline is to tell your population that you are starting a phishing program. Warn them. Basically you tell them you are going to start phishing; you explain that your goals are to create a more secure environment for the company and them personally and that you will be sending simulated phishing e-mails to them at X intervals.

I suggest that you even give them the actions you want them to take to

- Identify phishing e-mails
- Report phishing e-mails

When this type of preemptive warning shot is fired over the company, it can have great effect on helping the employees to know not only what is expected but also how to handle the program.

The Surprise Phish Baseline

The second philosophy for handling a phishing program is more aggressive. In this case you set a baseline with no warning shot. You launch a phishing e-mail against the company without any pre-education and see what the results are.

Why do some people choose this method? This method offers the clearest picture as to where your employees are in the world of real phishing attacks against them.

Some people choose to warn their employees because they want to give their people the best chance for taking every educational opportunity to remain vigilant.

Which method is the best? Honestly, I can't answer that for you. It depends on your culture, your people, your experience, and many other factors.

I can say, however, that both methods help you set a baseline, and both help you get your start into using phishing as an education tool for your population. My advice is to choose the one that suits you the best and then go from there.

After you've decided which baseline method to use, how do you know what type of phish to send?

Setting the Difficulty Level

Even if you get nothing else from this book, please pay attention to this section, as it is the crux of our program. The reason it is so important is that this is where you set the levels of the phish. Over the years I have cataloged phishing e-mails that I saw in the wild. When Michele and I started to work together, we created a phishing library that contains dozens of real-life examples that we've categorized in a system.

This system sets standards for phishing e-mails based on their difficulty level—that is, the level of complexity of the e-mail that determines how hard it is to detect that it is a phishing e-mail. Michele and I have broken these down into four levels that can literally encompass almost all base e-mails.

Let me walk you through these levels then discuss how you can utilize them.

Level One Phish

A level one phish is quite simple to catch. It is generally associated with a 419 scam e-mail (described in Chapter 1). There are *many* indicators of its "phishy-ness," and most average users should find it relatively easy to pick out that this e-mail just isn't right.

When Michele and I started to catalog these e-mails and picked out identifying characteristics, we were able to classify level one phish with these indicators:

- Impersonal greeting and closing
- Misspellings/bad grammar
- Easy message/improbable pretext (for example, "you've inherited millions")
- Appeals to sense of greed, fear, or curiosity
- Bad links in body
- Bad origin e-mail address/unknown sender

In most cases, a level one phish contains many of these indicators. Although you might not see as many of these types of e-mails in the wild as you used to, we provide a few examples:

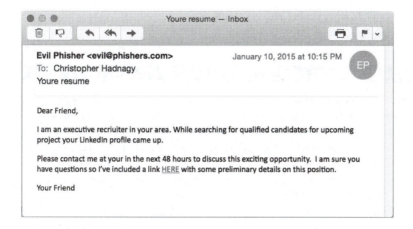

Level one phish seem almost silly when you read them here, but believe it or not they work. Remember Michele's section on influence? These e-mails work well because of fear and greed. The fear of potential loss, the feelings of greed, and the desire for the "what-if" outweigh logic and reasoning.

LEVEL ONE IN REAL LIFE

I once met with a guy who assisted in launching malicious attacks before he went "legit," and he told me a harrowing tale that will send shivers up your spine. Not only would this guy and his cohorts send these types of e-mails, but they would back them up with live people. Let me give you an example.

Say you're a sorry sap who responded to this type of e-mail. You receive a reply telling you that you need to sign legal papers, and an appointment has been set in an office in a city.

As you walk into the office, there is a man in a military uniform who appears to be from *<insert country of e-mail origin here>*, and he has a lot of legal-looking papers. You sign bank transfer forms, legal right forms, power of attorney forms—all of which feed into the pretext of the e-mail. Then you turn over a check for the minimal fee of $5,000. That seems like a small amount in exchange for the $4.5 million you're going to get later. Unfortunately, because of government problems, just one week later you're told that another $5,000 is needed to help release the funds from government hold.

My acquaintance told me that after taking victims for $5,000 to $15,000, he and his associates would just disappear. Doing this to 5, 10, 20, or 100 people at once was not a bad haul for a small group from a foreign country with a few operatives in the United States. In a month they could pull in $1 million to $4 million—yes, you read that right—and disappear into the sunset.

So the moral is that you shouldn't laugh and think a level one phish is so dumb it won't work. Remember when I told you I sent 3 million phish in the past year? Well, with a level one phish I still get a 5 percent to 7 percent click ratio, so, on the low end, that is 150,000 people who click that e-mail. All the phishers need is one person who's willing to click and open malware to ruin your network, so 150,000 isn't bad.

Level Two Phish

A level two phish has more complexity to it, and although it has many indicators similar to those of a level one phish, its themes are more sophisticated and harder to detect. Michele and I have identified these indicators:

- Impersonal greeting and closing
- Spelled properly with some bad grammar
- Messaging more complex but still basic
- Appeals to sense of greed, fear, or curiosity

- Bad links in body

- Bad origin e-mail address/unknown sender

As mentioned, there are many similarities to the level one phish, but one difference that we noticed is the theme. We see less of the "you are getting $4.5 million" theme, and we see more corporate- and personal-based e-mails that are using curiosity and fear as their motivators.

Take a look at a couple examples we have seen in the wild:

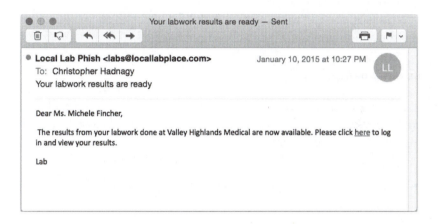

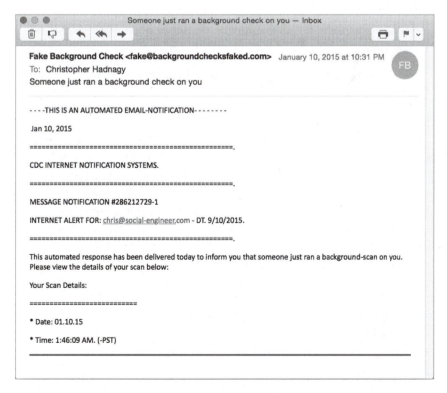

As you can see, these phish are playing more on a sense of curiosity and fear and trying to get the recipient to click a link that compromises his identity or the company's network.

In the first example, the name in the e-mail is wrong for the purpose of eliciting curiosity. If you received an e-mail like this, you might think, "Wait, I got Ms. Doe's medical lab records. I wonder what she went in for. Let me just take a peek."

The second example plays on the fear that someone might have discovered your deep, dark secrets.

In both cases, you feel motivated to click the link, open the attachment, or take the action you definitely should not take.

Level Three Phish

A level three phish is about as close to real-world targeted attacks as you will see outside of a spear phish (which is the top category). A level three phishing e-mail is complex and really hard to decipher.

Some of the indicators of a level three phish are as follows:

- Personalized greeting and closing
- Spelled properly
- Generally good grammar
- Complex message that appeals to a sense of fear or curiosity
- Bad links in body
- Sometimes a bad origin e-mail address, but sender can appear legitimate
- Branding in many cases

The key to a level three phish is that it looks and feels real. Even professionals may fall for them or need some time to truly decipher whether it's real or fake. The phish I spoke about previously that appeared to be from Amazon.com was a level three phish.

What we have been seeing more and more is that the messaging on this level is *not* geared toward fear. I'm not saying the attackers don't use fear—because they do—but we have been seeing an increase in other motivators such as greed, empathy, desire, and curiosity.

As I wrote this section, the news hit the web about another AT&T insider breach. Thousands of accounts are at risk, and as I was warning my family and friends about the potential phishing and vishing attacks, I received the message shown in Figure 5-2.

Figure 5-2: AT&T level three phish

Let's break down this e-mail by the characteristics I described earlier to see how smart and devious this phish is:

- **Personalized greeting and closing:** Although the e-mail is not personalized, imagine how someone who uses AT&T would feel about this e-mail. Like it was meant for her?

- **Spelled properly with generally good grammar:** You will be hard pressed to find misspellings and bad grammar here.

- **Complex message that appeals to a sense of fear or curiosity:** No fear here, just the curiosity of what kinds of deals there may be.

- **Bad links in body:** The links in the e-mail all appear to go to legitimate AT&T addresses, all *except* the main one, which goes to a false credential-harvesting page.

- **Sometimes a bad origin e-mail address, but sender can appear legitimate:** Did you notice the From address? That's definitely not a real AT&T address.

- **Branding in many cases:** This message is definitely branded to lend further credence to the e-mail's legitimacy.

This is a level three phish in the wild. Not many corporations or even pentesters will go to this level of phish. The branding in this phish is realistic and many of the links go to the legitimate site, so using this as a phish is surely to raise some eyebrows and more.

I had to share it with you because these types of attacks are increasingly in the news, and it literally came into my inbox as I was typing.

I also have an example of a level three e-mail that is used in legitimate corporate phishing programs.

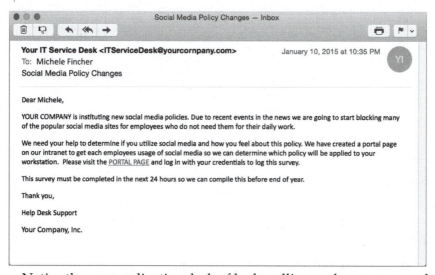

Notice the personalization, lack of bad spelling and grammar, and even the lack of branding of your company. This kind of an e-mail is very hard for many employees to catch. What is the one indicator of the phish?

The e-mail address. It is not `yourcompany.com` but `yourcoRNpany.com`. That subtle difference is very hard to catch, but if you train your people to look closely for these kinds of details, they can spot this one and not fall victim.

In a phishing program, this level phish is generally not used at the start with inexperienced companies; it's saved for more advanced folks.

Level Four Phish, or Spear Phish

This level is very advanced, very personal, and, many times, very successful. What's interesting about a level four or spear phish is that it may contain personalization, branding, no spelling errors, and the like. But it may also be the simplest e-mail on earth.

You might have heard about the RSA hack of 2011. That spear phish (see Figure 5-3) was sent to just a few people within that company.

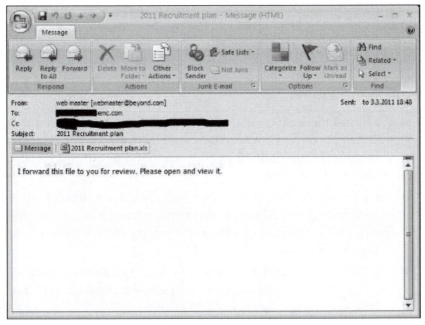

Figure 5-3: The K.I.S.S. principle in action

I know; it seems like anyone should be able to identify this phish, but the fact is that it worked. So did the simple one-line e-mail to Coca-Cola about the president's green initiative for Coke. It worked at the White House, too. The list can go on and on, but what all these situations have in common is they were simple and to the point. How did they work?

These attacks were effective because the people they were sent to were expecting a message of this type. They were ready to receive, accept, open, and read e-mails with this "theme." It made sense for them to receive an e-mail of this type; therefore, they complied with the request in the e-mail.

In many cases, the spear phish is more about the open-source intelligence (OSINT, or information gathering) portion of the attack than the e-mail portion. And that portion can lead an attacker to a clear path to the victim and knowledge of how to infiltrate the target.

In the case of the Coca-Cola company, after the link was clicked a slew of malware was loaded on the target's machine. The target's compromised machine therefore compromised the network.

In a corporate sense, our spear phishing work is usually preceded by OSINT. We give a report to the client that includes what intelligence we found, how it could be used, and the results of the spear phish that was sent.

Showing you some real examples of spear phish we have written would compromise our clients, so let me give you some themes and you can see how this works.

- We found the location of our clients' home and discovered that their neighbors' house was on the market. We presented the targets with a free home evaluation after we found out they were also going to list their home.

- After finding out that an exec loved to take his family on vacation and their favorite destination was Paris, we sent a spear advertising an enchanting tour of Paris in the spring that happened to be going on discount.

- After finding out that an exec graduated from a military school 24 years and 10 months ago, we formulated a phish inviting him to be a keynote speaker at his 25th reunion.

- After finding out that an exec's daughter "hated her dad," we sent an e-mail from a school counselor that included some details and a PDF report.

Are these terribly malicious? Yes, definitely. There's no doubt about the maliciousness of these themes. But if your execs hold the keys to your kingdom (and some we have worked with hold the keys to nuclear facilities or worse), this type of testing is imperative to educate people on the potential dangers and risks they are exposing themselves and your company to by not understanding how dangerous phishing is as a threat.

I would be remiss if I didn't take a few minutes to talk about another vector that falls under spear phishing level four attacks before moving on. That is the multi-tiered attack, which goes like this:

11:00 a.m. John receives an e-mail in his inbox.

11:35 a.m. John receives a call from "Larry in IT," who says, "John, this is Larry down in IT. I just sent you an e-mail with a PDF that is outlining the upgrade path for your workstation. I need you to open it and let me know if your machine fits these specs."

John says, "Umm, Larry? Ahhh, okay." John clicks the attachment and says, "Larry, it crashed and won't open."

Larry replies, "Dang, John, are you still using Acrobat 6.0? We were supposed to upgrade you two months ago. Okay, let me reprint it into an acceptable format. I will call you back right after lunch and send you a new file. Okay?"

John says, "Okay. Thanks, Larry," and hangs up.

In the meantime, "Larry" is hacking the network with the malware he planted on John's computer.

Here's another popular vector I have seen work: The attacker mails an exec a brand-new piece of hardware that has been embedded with malware devices. For example, my good friend David Kennedy created a keyboard with an embedded device that gives an attacker access to the corporate network after it has been plugged in.

How many execs do you think plug in the brand-new $200 Microsoft keyboard when they get it in the mail? One hundred percent.

These types of attacks are very targeted and very personal, and—instead of casting a wide net—they use a single spear to catch their prey. Many times this type of spear phishing is labeled as "whaling," or going after the "big fish" in the company.

This defines the levels of our program, but now the next logical question is, how do you choose where to start?

Choose Your Level Carefully

What level should you choose to start off your phishing program? This question is actually easier to answer than you may think, and there are two different camps to phish in:

■ **Camp one:** Start with bass before you go for the marlin. This means that you should start with the smaller phish—these are your level one attacks. See how your population does, and move through all difficulty levels in level one, then move to level two. Start as easy as you can, then move up.

■ **Camp two:** Deep sea phishing for the big phish. This means starting with the level three attacks and then ramping backward until you hit a moderate level and work from there.

How do you choose? Well, I generally like to phish in camp one. I think it promotes a better feeling with the population. They feel like they are getting a win, and that helps them to adopt the program more easily. Is it the best way of going? I won't say it is the best for security, but I can say it is the best when it comes to keeping people happy and invested in your security program.

I also factor in experience and the length of the program. Here are a few scenarios I have been in and how I decided to proceed:

■ **Company One:** A company asked me to run its phishing program. The company had never used phishing in its awareness program before, but the leaders knew it was a problem and wanted only one phish every quarter.

I decided to start at the low end of level two, phish the entire population in Q1, and educate and move them all up to a harder level two attack in Q2. We continued to educate and then moved up to a low-end level three attack in Q3. We saw a significant increase in the click rate, as well as a slight increase in the reporting ratio. So in Q4 we stayed at a low-end level three attack. The click ratio went down. The continual education and testing seemed to work well with this company.

■ **Company Two:** We were again asked to run the program. They already had been phishing for one year on their own, had very low click ratios, and had buy-in from the higher-ups for the program.

We phished the whole population each month. We started at a moderate level two attack and moved up each month. By the fourth month we were at a moderate level three attack. We saw an increasing number of clicks, but every subsequent month, there were more people catching the phish.

As you can see, where you begin depends on many factors. Keep this short list of questions in mind:

- Have you phished before?
- Do you have solid buy-in from the management levels above you (the ones who can stop the program)?
- How often will you phish?
- Are you phishing the whole population?

Writing the Phish

You have your baselines; you have chosen your level; everyone has bought in; and you are ready to start phishing. If you are running this program yourself and using a phishing tool to do so, you might be tempted to just go grab a template from the software and click Send.

Before you go jumping on the phish wagon, Captain Clickity Clicky Click, let's discuss some ideas that can help you pick the perfect phish.

It is true that some of the templates in these software packages are good. But will they work for your company? Your answers to the questions throughout this chapter should give you a clear picture of what type of phish you want (for example, branded or not, personal or not, corporate or not).

Then you have to decide also how to best help your population. Let me illustrate it this way. I am usually all for the realism. I like to grab something from the headlines and use it to really help people see what the bad guys will do. In one case, it was about two or three years after September 11 when the planes hit the towers in New York City, and we were approaching the anniversary of that event.

There were dozens of charities all over the web that were calling for help and donations. I wrote a phish that was all about the events for a fake charity. I was really proud of myself; it looked real, sounded real, and would have gotten all sorts of emotions involved.

I sent it to HR to review before we scheduled sending it, and the HR department rejected it. I couldn't understand why, so we had a meeting. In the company, more than a handful of people had lost brothers, sisters, fathers, and friends in those attacks. How would those people have felt if their company authorized the use of that tragedy to teach a lesson?

I can hear your moans and sighs of disbelief now. "But the bad guys will do that, so people need to learn!" I agree with the sentiment, but the fact remains that I am *not* the bad guy. I care about my clients; I care about their feelings and their people. I don't want to send a phish that will cause permanent emotional damage. We never sent that phish, and I learned my lesson.

Now here's another story from the opposite perspective. I once sent a phishing e-mail that was a very low-end level two. The gist was something like, "Thank you for switching your credit card's e-mail address to attacker@hack.com." It was more eloquent than that, but that was the basic premise.

We sent it to tens of thousands of people. Many were upset, but most quickly got over it. One woman got so upset about the e-mail, though, that she cancelled all her credit cards, moved her bank accounts, and responded to the e-mail address in the phish with a near death threat.

In this case, I took a different stance than I did with the September 11 example. This woman clicked the link, which led her to an education page, and even after seeing the education page, she still decided to cancel her accounts and cards instead of taking the actions she had been taught to take (such as calling her IT department). Had she done what she had been taught, she would have saved herself a lot of heartache.

For your program, decide what level of phish you want, then write a few that have the defining principles I outlined earlier, meet with your phishing brain trust, and work on the phish to perfect them.

WARNING   Remember, you *know* it's a phish, and because you do, the signs will always seem to be too easy to spot. Don't assume that because you see it so clearly that everyone else will. Be willing to go easier in the beginning.

Tracking and Statistics

A considerable amount of Chapter 7 covers the software offerings for phishing tracking. It is important to have in mind what software and features you want because what you choose to use can affect the data you can collect. There is a massive difference between buying some marketing e-mail software to just capture a rough idea of who clicks e-mails and using a robust SaaS (Software as a Service) solution that tracks every ounce of detail you can ever want.

I won't spend time here on the choices, but I will say this: Deciding what statistics and data you want from your program can help you make the choice of what to use.

At this point, you might have a flawless program, but without the best data it is useless, right? Here is where we have found the major difference between minor-league phishers and the pros (I'm talking those who do this as a service to help companies).

The simple difference is the statistics they collect and what they mean to the company. I can hear a few people right now saying, "All we need is click ratio, right?" WRONG!

Click ratio is important. But if I send you a few level one phish and your click ratio is, say, 10 percent, and in month three I send you a level three phish and the click ratio goes to 90 percent . . . well, click ratio will basically make it look like your population suddenly became phishing stupid. Yet that is not the case in this scenario.

Recall the reason for this program: to educate your population on how to recognize, report, and defend against phishing e-mails. What statistics will give the guys with the checkbook the warm and fuzzy feeling that they are spending money in the right place? How do you set up the program to maximize this benefit? What can statistics tell you about your program to help you improve? I have answers to all these questions.

Just the Stats, Ma'am

As I mentioned earlier, you have to first decide what data is important to you and then decide where to go from there. Many times I've been asked what I consider to be important data. Before I break down the statistics we collect and tell you why each is important, let's think about what makes a star employee when it comes to phishing. You know that clicking is bad and not clicking is good. That is simple enough—but what about other good and bad behaviors?

Hopefully you have a reporting agency for your population in your organization. Employees reporting any phishing e-mail they catch to the proper "authorities" in your company can save lots of heartache and even a breach or two. So employees who report phishing e-mails go on the good list.

I'm also frequently asked how employees should report. The best suggestion is to have them forward the phishing e-mail to a certain inbox in the department that handles this task. That forwarded mail can be analyzed and then the employees can be advised about what they should do. I have had companies suggest a phone number for reporting, but imagine you have 5,000 employees, 50 percent of whom call to report phishing e-mails, and those people are getting one e-mail each per day. Talk about a stressful job that will lead nowhere.

Here are the statistics I find to be important:

- **Number of people who clicked:** This is the obvious statistic, but it's necessary. It is your baseline. It is the number that tells you how many people may put the company at risk and how many people need to be further educated. However, this statistic alone doesn't tell you much. You need to build on it.

- **Number of people who reported the phish:** I am making an assumption here, and that assumption is that your company has a reporting agency for its employees to report phishing e-mails to. This is such an important part of "fixing" the phishing problem. Our goal is to create an environment where all employees are reporting the e-mails as soon as they see them, before they click. The truth is that you also need to teach your employees what to do "when" they click. Deleting is not a good answer; they need an agency to report to. Many times when I start working with a company, the first thing I have to do is help it set up this agency, but it is a vital step.

  Let's get back to the assumption that you have a reporting agency. One of the statistics you need from every phishing campaign is how many people "caught" the phish and reported it to that agency. I will cover some methods on how to track this in a bit.

- **Number of people who clicked and didn't report:** You know clicking is bad and reporting is good, so in this case employees who click but do not report took both actions you do *not* want them to take. These employees need the most training and help.

- **Number of people who clicked and did report:** Understanding that people clicked the e-mail and still reported it is a great statistic. Why? This means that although those people took the one action you don't want, they had been educated to realize risk is still there and took the positive step to report it.

- **Number of people who did not click and did not report:** Because the employees in this category don't click, the danger isn't there for breach. However, you still want the people who don't click to report that they've received something suspicious. Reporting is the step that every employee needs to understand the importance of.

- **Number of people who did not click and did report:** People in this category are your star employees. They took both actions that you wanted them to take. Not only did they catch the phish, but they also reported it to save others.

Because you know that employees who need the most help are those who clicked and did not report and that the star employees are those who did not click and did report, you want to track the numbers from those categories to hopefully see the number in the latter group increasing with each campaign, which would demonstrate that your hard work is paying off.

There are many ways to track these statistics, but I have found that helping the IT/Help Desk (or whatever department is managing the phishing program) set up some rules can make this task easier.

For example, we sometimes embed text in the e-mail that matches the background color (white); we ingeniously call this text the "white text." (I know; *where* do I come up with this brilliant stuff?) The text needs to include characters that would never be used in a normal sentence— something like `Th1$i$aphi$hingemail0rz-DATEHERE`.

Then we set a rule that tells the reporting mailbox to filter any e-mail that is forwarded to it to a special folder—something like `Oct201X Phishing Reporters`. Unless your SaaS/ solution has a method to help you track it (more on that in Chapter 7), you grab this list at the end of the month and use some easy Excel kung fu to quickly compare that list to the list of those who clicked, didn't click, and so on. Voilà, you have your statistics!

We have even implemented some robust features of that special inbox that specify that if the rule is initiated, the senders get a thank-you e-mail telling them they caught the phish and they did a good job reporting it.

However you decide to do it, the earlier lists of stats are the ones that can give you a clear picture of where you stand, how to improve, and where you need to work with your phishing program.

Reporting

All the hard work of setting up a program comes down to this: the report. This is the document that takes the hours of hard work, sweat, tears, blood, decisions, and more tears and rolls it all into the reason why every bit of it was worthwhile.

This is not a how-to section on report writing. I'm just briefly describing how we report the statistics because it may spark some ideas for you.

Let's use CompanyX. CompanyX has 1,000 employees, and it wanted us to phish them every month. They have never phished before, and they don't want external branding. They want to use internal branding but only after they start their program with level one phish and see where to grow from there.

My report would contain a chart like the following:

MONTH ONE: LEVEL 1	NUMBER	STATISTIC
E-mails Sent	1000	100%
Number Clicked	750	75%
Number Reported	50	5%
Click / No Report	705	70.5%
Clicked / Report	45	4.5%
No Click / No Report	15	1.5%
No Click / Report	5	0.5%

Of course there would be graphs and supporting text around it. In month two, we phish again. We report the same statistics we did in month one, but we also note the change between months one and two.

MONTH TWO: LEVEL 1	NUMBER	STATISTIC	CHANGE
E-mails Sent	1000		
Number Clicked	600	60%	-15%
Number Reported	350	35%	30%
Click / No Report	350	35%	-35.5%
Clicked / Report	250	25%	20.5%
No Click / No Report	13	1.3%	-0.2%
No Click / Report	100	10%	9.50%

Of course, I could keep listing months, but you get the point. In one month you can show that your program helped to not only reduce the number of clicks by 15 percent but also increase the number of reported phish by 30 percent. Diving deeper you can show that your education is working, as the group who most need training was reduced by 35.5 percent, and the number of star employees in the No Click/Report category went up by 9.5 percent.

This type of reporting helps the executives see that you are doing a good job and that the program is well worth the investment of time and money.

Now, what if your numbers don't go like this? What if you see star employee numbers drop? Ask yourself these questions:

- Did I just bump up a level? It is possible that moving from level one to two—or from two to three—can cause momentary loss in numbers until you train the employees at that level. Don't despair just yet.

- Were there holidays or vacations during the campaign? Sometimes we see spikes or drops in numbers, and it is simply that people are not there or lack focus.

- Is my education working? Analyze your educational piece. Is it too long, too wordy, or too demeaning? The education must balance being quick, simple, and effective.

Whatever the reason, don't get terribly concerned unless you see these numbers increasing month after month in the wrong direction.

Now, let's talk a little more about that last bullet: education.

Phish, Educate, Repeat

The education portion of this campaign is one of the biggest portions of your program. Let's go back to the cooking analogy: You buy the best ingredients. You cook everything to perfection. You seat your guests. Your plating is marvelous. You put the plates down in front of your guests and . . . they have no utensils.

The utensils help you get the most out of your amazing meal. With them you take the food in and more easily get nourishment from it. In your phishing program, the education is your utensil. It is imperative to have utensils that work and are right for the job.

Imagine putting down a beautiful bowl of fish chowder for your guests and then giving them a butter knife. Your education (the utensil) has to fit the meal and the guests.

We approach education with what we call the BEST method:

- **Brief:** Long computer-based training that bores your employees will do nothing to effectively teach them. Something that takes them one to four minutes to complete is the most efficient.

- **Effective:** Teach the employees *how* they could have caught the phish, *what* to do when they see another, and *where* to report it.

- **Simple:** If the training uses terminology employees are not familiar with, or it is overly complicated in telling them what to do, your staff will feel frustrated. That frustration will have a negative effect on the training.

- **Thoughtful:** Do you understand how much work your people do each day? The pressures they are under? If you do, then you will thoughtfully prepare the best training possible so you are not adding stress to their already busy lives. Yet at the same time, you are preparing them to protect themselves, their families, and your company from phishing attacks. How thoughtful of you!

I have seen some well-intentioned folks try to overly complicate this BEST method, and it has the reverse effect—instead of educating and inspiring your people, it can frustrate and confuse them. If you stick with the BEST method as described here, you'll generally have good results. For example, in one company we work with, we have seen an average click ratio of 89 percent with less than 10 percent reporting improve to an average of 7 percent click ratio with 75 percent reporting using the very methods I have outlined in this chapter.

Of course the final step of this whole program is to *repeat it*. Don't think once-a-year phishing will protect your people.

Let me ask you a question; you need to answer honestly. You have less than five seconds from when you read this next sentence to spit out your answer:

> Name the three top points from last year's security awareness session . . . GO.

If you were honest, you probably stared at the page for a bit, and you maybe came up with one answer. But you probably didn't get all three or even come close. Yet five seconds is a long time when it comes to how fast your people need to react when a phishing e-mail is in front of them. Don't expect them to be able to recall all the training you gave them if the last time they saw it was a year ago. Or, if I'm your employee, don't expect me to remember if it was more than 45 days ago.

Summary

After reading this chapter you might be thinking, "Wow, this is too much work. I will just take my chances." I won't lie; the initial set up is a bit of work. Sometimes getting buy-in from the executive floor, HR, legal, and other departments can take a good fight. Launching the program and not having everyone hate you might also be a small battle. But time after time when we have helped companies get this program going, we have seen the rewards.

One company reported a 70 percent reduction in malware incidents related to e-mail. Seventy percent!!! That alone makes it all worthwhile.

Employees of that company can hate me if they want, but 70 percent of them are not getting the malware they would have a year ago.

Phishing is here to stay because it is easy, effective, and profitable for the malicious attacker. Vigilance and fortitude are required on your part to get this program going and to make it the best it can be.

Before we can move on to helping you with your software choice, there is one more topic that has to be covered. That is the topic of policies. Now wait, before you go flipping past that chapter, take a moment to think about what you can learn from reviewing the good, the bad, and the ugly in policies. See you there.

The Good, the Bad, and the Ugly: Policies and More

"The educated don't get that way by memorizing facts; they get that way by respecting them."

—Tom Heehler

Policy seems like a four-letter word to some people. I almost wanted to wipe that word from this book, but Michele and I quickly realized that if we didn't discuss the examples we have, the methods that we have witnessed employed, and the decisions we have helped either make or combat, then this book would be flawed.

Why is understanding how to implement policies so important? Many of the very things you read in this chapter start off sounding good, and we understand why many companies think they might work. Also, we have learned a thing or five from our customers and want to help you by sharing what we've learned.

When we pondered the best way to do this, we thought about breaking it down into sections about the good, the bad, and the ugly . . . but quickly my list was leaning heavy to the bad and ugly sides of the scale, so we decided to change the methodology on this.

Instead I want to present each idea or policy and then discuss it from three angles:

- What is the definition of the policy, idea, or thought?
- Why it is bad or ugly?
- And then finally, how can it be made "good"?

My hope is not to make anyone feel bad but to merely help you think through why these policies might not work and how they can be modified to make a positive effect in your phishing program.

Let's get started.

Oh, the Feels: Emotion and Policies

When I was about 17 I started working out pretty regularly. (I know . . . what happened?) Because I was young, active, and determined, I packed on some serious muscle—fast.

Time passed, and I continued working out. As I got older, one day I found myself in the gym with a group of avid weight lifters. They were packing the plates on the bar, and—not wanting to seem weaker— I proclaimed I could "of course" do the same weight.

Down I lay on the bench, and as the weight descended I realized I had made a mistake, but I writhed, wriggled, grunted, pushed, and got the weight back up. One rep. And I was the big man on campus. Across the gym was a trainer who witnessed my utter display of idiocy. After a short while he invited me over to his bench. He had a couple small plates on the bar and asked me to bench with him. Arrogantly, I referred to my previous victory and said this weight was just warm-up weight for me. He lay down on the bench as I spotted for him and bumped out a machine-quality, slow, articulate set of 10 reps of this weight. He asked, "Would you allow me to teach you the right way to bench?"

He talked to me about form, arm placement, back arch, and all the things I was doing wrong. I lay down and barely did a set of five reps using the proper form before I was back to arching my wriggling back. He corrected me, and I tried again. After weeks of practice, I was a benching machine. Sure, I was using less weight, but I was a machine.

After a few sessions I found myself with my buddies again and noticed they were benching perfectly. I asked them why they hadn't told me that I was totally screwing up, and they simply said, "Well, you were doing it; we didn't want to discourage ya." Thankfully that trainer had the guts to teach me the right way of doing it, as it changed my whole life (well, my whole workout life).

The Definition

Let me just set this fact straight: You do have to care about your people, and you have to take into consideration their feelings and how they will react to your phish.

With that said, this one policy rule centers on a company that puts too much weight on that fact. Yes, you must care about your people, but will that stop you from realistic phishing because you don't want *anyone* to be upset? Will you hold back from pointing out their "wrong form" because you're trying to avoid some hurt feelings?

Will you limit the breadth and scope of your phishing attempts because you are worried that your employees will be too upset by the content of the phish? We have seen companies who use level one phish and stay at that level (or even use easier phish) so they can say they are giving phishing education, but they never really challenge their employees to learn how to recognize real phish.

The Bad

The notion of putting everyone's feelings in front of good education is a bad one because it limits the education you give your population. Let me illustrate this with my weight-lifting scenario. Building muscle required a combination of breaking down the muscle I had using the right form and proper weights, recovering and growing, then repeating the process. You can't break down muscle by lifting weight that is too easy for you. In the same fashion you can't build phishing muscle without first breaking down what you have.

Making It "Good"

To properly build your phishing muscle, you need to increase the "weight" of the phish as time passes. With that said, you don't have to go full bore and not have any regard for people's feelings, but the phish need to be realistic.

I agree with avoiding themes that may be so personal it can cause people to feel damaged or violated, but how close can you push it to the line without going that far? I can't answer that for you here; it's something you need to analyze and determine on your own.

The Boss Is Exempt

"I learned it from watching you!" My friends and I must have used those words more than a million times when we were joking with each other. Those words that we jokingly used were from a very serious public service announcement (PSA) from the Partnership for a Drug-Free America (1987). In the PSA, a young man is being questioned by his father because the son's mother had found a box of drugs in the closet.

As the father is scolding his son and asking, "Who taught you how to use this stuff?" the son finally caves in and yells those infamous words that defined 1987: "You, alright! I learned it from watching you."

The PSA highlighted a key point that's relevant for all of us: You are not exempt from the rules just because you happen to believe you sit higher on the food chain than the next guy.

The Definition

When we take an engagement to help a company start a phishing program, we work hard to get the boss's approval. It's common that we get the green light to proceed after submitting 10 proposals, attending 50 meetings, and sending a few hundred e-mails. When it takes that much effort to get the ball rolling, we know the whole program is on a thin thread of acceptance.

Because our contacts at the company don't want anything to stop us from proceeding with the program, they sometimes say, "We are gonna just leave the C-level execs out of these tests." After we spend a few moments in puzzled bewilderment, they may even add, "They don't need it as much."

Sigh.

The Bad

It is most likely obvious to you why it is so bad to leave the C-level executives out of a phishing program, but let me explain it anyway. Think back to that 1987 commercial: "I learned it from watching you!"

That PSA includes an important lesson: Proper actions and attitudes come from the top down. If your C-level is not willing to be tested with the rest of the population, what message does that send?

Making It "Good"

On the flip side, when the boss is 100 percent invested in the program, the attitude of your population can be drastically altered to be positive and accepting. When the staff sees that the top level willingly accepts the program and is being tested, everyone else doesn't feel singled out.

One company tackled this issue by the president writing an e-mail to the company stating his support for the program. He even shared his first month's click ratio from the phishing test. When the employees saw not only that the president was on board with the program but that he failed the first e-mail, they felt good about the program and also the support from the company. In this case, it's a good thing if one of the employees says, "I learned it from watching you. . . ."

I'll Just Patch One of the Holes

When I was younger I used to be an avid surfer. I had this really old board I used to ride when the waves were really small. It was thick enough and big enough to catch a dolphin's burp. Like most youths, I didn't appreciate the value of the things I had, so I tossed that board around a lot.

After a few months of abuse, the board had a few dings—one on the underside and one on the rail (or side)—that needed to be fixed. The waves were supposed to be up the next day, so I didn't want to spend too much time with repairs. I slapped some resin and fiberglass on the ding on the underside.

I looked at the rail and rationalized, "This is going to require a lot of sanding. What if it doesn't set in time? Then I won't be able to surf." I grabbed some wax and duct tape and did a quick repair.

Happy with myself and feeling secure, I paddled out the next day. After a few hours I noticed a bubble under the fiberglass of the deck that was "squishy."

Sure enough—the quick repair job on the rail didn't hold up. As the sun beat down, the wax heated and moved. Water got in, and the board became waterlogged—heavy, waterlogged, and ruined. I didn't catch many waves that day.

The Definition

Maybe it's due to budget. Maybe it's due to wrong reasoning. Maybe it's due to a bad consultant. Whatever the reason, choosing to test only part of the population is like patching only one out of two dings.

Phishing is so subjective and people based that you can't test only a portion of the population and say, "Well, this 30 percent that we tested has a 10 percent click ratio, so we are doing great," or "They have a 90 percent click ratio; everyone is doomed. . . ."

Remember, it takes only *one* click to compromise your network. Can you really take the chance that malicious attackers will hit only your tested employees?

The Bad

How susceptible people are to phishing and responsive to education is dependent very much on each person. Choosing random numbers of employees or a small subset of the population does not do much to tell you how your company as a whole will fair under attack.

Also, if the people chosen to be tested are those who are already aware of the program or of phishing, it can lead you to a false sense of security by enabling you to think your company is more prepared than it is.

Making It "Good"

I can't fix budget issues, and having something is better than having nothing. I generally think that doing very little as opposed to being all in is not good, but having a small program may be a necessity in some cases. However, if it is not a necessity to take smaller bites, then just don't do it. Testing a small sample is not good for your company, and the last thing you want is to end up "waterlogged" and phished.

Let's say that you can get approval for only a one-time phish. I understand you gotta do what you gotta do, but the stats from that one time should not be used to say how secure you are. Instead you should use them to show what needs to be done next quarter or year. In that case, I think it can be a powerful tool to get a baseline. But a single test like this, if it must be done, should be viewed strictly as a baseline.

Phish Just Enough to Hate It

Did you ever do something just enough to hate it? I remember when I first started learning to speak another language. I did just enough to learn the bare minimum and avoided the homework like it was a bad word. Therefore, I didn't progress as fast as I wanted and was disappointed and frustrated when presented with a test or a question in that language. I constantly wanted to give up.

What was happening? I was doing it just enough to say, "I am taking this language," but I wasn't doing enough to really learn. Therefore I suffered the anxiety and frustration that comes with being a new learner well past the time I should have been feeling that way.

The Definition

At first your company may approach phishing like fraud awareness training or locking your laptop up when at Starbucks. If you've ever sat through that training you know what I mean. The instructor tells you a few dozen ways why something is bad, shows you a short video on how to do it right, and hopes you learned something. If it is viewed that way, it is possible that the training will be viewed as something that can be handled as a "one-and-done" type of training.

The sad reality is that, as we mentioned before, each of us are most likely getting handfuls of phishing e-mails per day. Testing employees once and giving them one-time training on how to recognize phish would be no different than giving them one lesson in French before sending them to France for a month—not very effective.

The Bad

I've seen the following results from the one-and-done type of thinking:

- **Extreme frustration:** For both the employees who feel like they are never progressing and the company that feels it is wasting money because no one is learning, frustration is the feeling du jour (see what I did there?) when this type of thinking is used.

- **Lack of awareness:** Not only is the training ineffective, but due to the aforementioned frustration, many employees do worse with recognizing phishing e-mails than those people who are consistently tested and educated.

- **Disconnect between IT and other employees:** The relationship between the IT department and the rest of the staff becomes more adversarial rather than being a "team" that's working together to support your interests.

- **Lack of metrics:** This may seem like a no-brainer, but the facts are that when a one-time program is implemented, the company lacks the proper metrics to prove that money was well spent and there is any effect from training.

Instead of helping, a single test seems to have the reverse effect. It actually hinders a company's ability to train its employees to be phishing resilient.

Making It "Good"

Okay, so I get it … not every company wants to send every employee one phish each month. Yes, I can argue 'til I am blue in the face that this is the best method and is proven to help, but there will still be many who want to start off slower. So, what is important to focus on?

Consistency and commitment. The training must be consistent—at least once per quarter or once every other month. And you must commit to it. Don't leave some employees out because you assume one department is too busy, too important, or too aware to be trained. Include all your people and see how they do with one phish every two months or one phish per quarter.

From there you can determine whether you should increase the frequency and figure out how you can work with your fellow employees as a team and not as an adversary.

Let's address budgetary constraints, too. It seems like resistance is the result of one of the following two things (or a combination of them):

- C-level execs that don't understand or buy in to the program
- An inability to provide numbers that show the investment will be worth it

Arguing against budgetary constraints is always a hard battle because it's like paying for insurance: You pay to avoid a negative as opposed to enjoying a positive.

If You Spot a Phish, Call This Number

I once volunteered to do demolition on a large building. The inside of the building was to be gutted so it could be rebuilt. The problem: It was all cinder-block walls.

I was brand new to demolition, but I was younger then and very strong. I grabbed a sledgehammer, the heaviest I could find, went into a room, and started smashing away at the wall. Shards of concrete block were flying everywhere, and I felt like a big man as I was smashing through this wall. After 15 minutes, I had created a gaping hole in the center of the wall; it was big enough that I could stick my head through.

I kept pounding and pounding until eventually I was so tired I needed a break. I went across the hall where this other guy was knocking down a whole wall. He had started working at the same time I had. Why was he so much farther along?

"Heck, no!!" I thought as I ran back to smash away at my wall. In a short time I had made another hole all the way through. As satisfying as it was to smash through whole block, I was nowhere near taking out the whole wall, and the other guy was on his second. I did the walk of shame over to his room and asked him for his secret.

He gave me a five-minute lesson on how rebar runs through walls at its weakest parts. He then told me where to hit and what size sledge to use. He gave me a pair of rebar cutters and sent me packing.

No more than 10 minutes later I was knocking down my first wall—and was that satisfying! By the end of the day we had two teams of two people competing to see who could knock down walls faster. And we had cleared a whole floor of every wall in a mere six-hour day—BY HAND!!

The Definition

The lesson I learned from the demolition story is that you should take the easiest path to success. Sure, the method I was using would have worked eventually, but it was not the easiest path to getting the job done.

Sometimes in companies we see very well-intentioned people making horrible decisions about how to get their people to take the right actions. This proves to be especially true when it comes to the reporting of phishing e-mails. We have seen too many companies set up internal call centers for employees to call to report all phishing e-mails that are caught. Whatever you decide, make it easy for your people to report to get the maximum benefit from them.

The Bad

You want your people to report any incident of phishing they "catch." You want your people to also wait to get more information on those e-mails before they take action. And you want to encourage the good behaviors that foster security-minded thinking.

However, if every time an employee gets a phish he has to call a number, report by voice all the details, and then be told to delete the e-mail, forward the e-mail, wait for more information, or ignore that e-mail, eventually the employee will stop reporting because doing so adds minutes or even hours to his workweek, and he just can't afford that time cost.

It's like asking your employees to pound away at the wall with the heaviest sledgehammer because it "feels" like they are getting something done, when it essence the program is really just tiring everyone out.

Making It "Good"

In every case that we have seen of companies successfully implementing phishing programs, reporting is handled via e-mail or web form to the appropriate team. In some cases, the responses on phishing tests are automated, and in very robust circumstances I have seen companies create phishing libraries that provide employees with comparisons for phish that have been received.

Either way, when reporting is easier on the employees, the employees' desire to report goes up, and their phishing education acceptance also goes up. I know: The goal is not just to make employees' lives easy. But people are busy, and—although social-engineering security is the most important thing in my mind—I realize that not everyone is on the same plane as me. You need to work with your people to make education something they want to participate in.

The Bad Guys Take Mondays Off

When I was a kid, my brother and I shared a room, and we had some cool bunk beds. One day my brother told me that giant rats would come out of the wall and eat me at midnight on a night with a full moon.

Before I closed my eyes at night I did my safety checks. Was there a full moon? If no, I was safe, and the time on the clock didn't matter. If yes, it was time to worry. A couple nights went by and I was "safe."

But one night as we were getting all tucked in and ready for sleep, I opened the curtain and peeked outside. "Oh no!" I thought. "It's a full moon!"

I looked at the clock and it was only 9:00 p.m. "What if I fall asleep? What if I am passed out at midnight, and the giant rats eat me in my sleep?!"

I stayed awake and stared at that clock for hours. Right around 11:55 p.m., my brother started scratching on the wall from his top bunk. I was frozen with fear. Precisely at midnight a hand reached down the side of the bunk and grabbed my neck. I let out a shriek that was probably heard a few states over.

I do believe there was many a beating shortly after that. Regardless, it took me some time to realize the following:

- There were no giant rats.

- If the giant rats had existed, they would not have waited until midnight when there was a full moon to eat me.

That lesson didn't make much sense when I was five or six, but there is so much application for it now.

The Definition

I have heard companies state an equivalent to my fanciful childhood fear. Not about giant rats, but about malicious phish. How so?

I have been told, "We want to run this phishing program, but Monday is too inconvenient, so we will never phish on Monday." Or, "Thursdays are staff meetings, so you can phish anytime you want, just not Thursdays." In essence, "It is okay to phish, just don't do it during a full moon."

Limiting the days or times you allow your phishing campaigns to run is like being convinced that giant rats who want to eat you only come out at midnight when there's a full moon. We all know that giant rats come out whenever they are hungry—not just at midnight. Seriously.

Similarly, the bad guys don't attack you only on days when you don't have your staff meetings.

The Bad

In companies where we have avoided specific days for testing, I have seen employees give the following type of response on surveys: "Well, I knew it wasn't our test phish because I got it on a Monday. We never get tested on Monday."

The goal, remember, is to train your people how to spot *all* phish *all the time*. You don't want them to figure out which phish are from you and which are from the bad guys. You want to make them more secure, safe, and phish-free no matter where they are or what day it is. You don't want to teach them that on Mondays and Thursdays they are safe from company-based phish.

Making It "Good"

The fix is obvious: Don't base your phishing dates on what is "convenient"; instead, base it on what is realistic in the attacker's mind. I agree that there are times that are just silly to phish. For example, times when everyone is on holiday or vacations or other times when there is a large part of the population that's not around. You want to have metrics and stats that assist in giving you a clear picture, so that means you want to phish when the people are there.

Realize, though, that phishers will not simply give you a break because you are having a holiday or a bad day. Remember, some of the most malicious phish that worked were sent shortly after the incident in New York City on 9/11, the tsunami that hit Japan, the earthquake in Haiti, and the hurricane that hit New Orleans. Phishers don't care about your suffering or the suffering of any other human; they care about getting their payday at any cost.

We are not the bad guys, so we do take into consideration your people and their feelings, but regularly excluding a day or two of the week due to meetings is not helping anyone.

If You Can't See It, You Are Safe

Here is yet another embarrassing story from my childhood. This one involves the boogeyman. We have all been scared of something—the noise in the closet, the bump under the bed, the branch hitting the window, or the shadow that looked like the boogeyman. No matter what the fear, it can cause irrational thought and actions. (True story: Michele used to run down the hallway holding a pillow on her back because it protected her from the dark.)

See, when I heard noises or thought I saw that thing moving in the closet, my idea was to freeze, get under the blankets, and close my eyes.

Why? Well, it's logical isn't it? If I can't see the monster/boogeyman/bad guy, then obviously I am safe. I equated safety to my ability to see the item that scared me.

Now that I am a fully qualified adult who realizes most of those fears were irrational, I also realize that if there was a real monster coming for me, covering myself with a blanket and closing my eyes would not so much have saved me as merely made me not see the object of my demise.

The Definition

Bad, scary e-mails come into your employees' inboxes—the question is, what's to be done with them? By now, I am sure you are aware I am going to promote a reporting program. But in cases where a company has not developed a reporting program, I have seen some companies suggest that employees should delete these e-mails as the solution to phishing.

For those of you who understand security, it is appalling to hear that "delete it" is the brand of security anyone would employ, but it does happen.

The Bad

What if the employee clicks the link, something crashes, they are now afraid, but the security advice is to delete the e-mail?

Even worse, what if the employee clicks the link, enters some credentials and then nothing happens, so the employee deletes the e-mail? A few days later the employee tells someone about it and now the security team wants to investigate, but the e-mail has been deleted forever.

What if the employee clicks the attachment and opens it to see the PDF reader crash? Afraid about what he clicked, he deletes the e-mail and now can't tell you which file crashed or even where it came from.

All of these scenarios are actual events I have witnessed firsthand at companies that suggested "deleting" as the answer.

Deleting e-mail is no different than burying your head under some blankets and thinking that you're safe because you can't see the bad thing.

Making It "Good"

There really is no improvement that doesn't involve some time and effort. You need a place for your employees to report suspicious e-mails. A place they can forward them so they can be reviewed. Without that, what is left? They can leave it, delete it, or click it.

The only improvement is to create the path you want your employees to take. After you clearly define that path, make sure it does a few things:

- Keeps your company safe
- Keeps your employees safe
- Protects the data and assets you worked hard to build

If your system accomplishes all those things, then it is an improvement over simply deleting the message and hoping for the best.

The Lesson for Us All

I can guarantee you that when each one of these policies was put in place it sounded like a great idea. Have you ever seen a commercial that's so bad you sit and wonder to yourself, "Wow. Someone actually paid for that." You imagine the marketing people sitting around the conference table high-fiving each other for the amazing idea that will revolutionize the market and how their product is sold.

I imagine a similar scenario happens when some of the policies in this chapter are developed when the motivator is stress, anxiety, and being over worked rather than a desire to be revolutionary. In addition, inexperience and a lack of good education on how to handle phishing e-mails go a long way into creating an environment where these ideas might seem like good ones.

Ask yourself these questions again to see if the policy you want to implement is good, bad, or ugly.

- What is the definition of the policy, idea, or thought?
- Why it is bad or ugly?
- How can it be made "good"?

Now let's take those answers and get some food for thought:

- Figure out your perfect path. What is it you want the employees to do? Do you want them to not click the e-mail and also report it? Do you want them to save the e-mail and report it? Forward the e-mail? Call in about it?
- Does this new policy really keep your *company* safe if your employees click or if they open the attachment?
- Does this new policy keep your *employees* safe if they click or if they open the attachment?

Answering these questions with regard to any of the policies described in this chapter would quickly illuminate whether they fall into the bad and ugly categories.

Summary

Policy is not a fun topic, and no one wants to spend their days making rules for everyone to follow. But they are essential for keeping your company safe, keeping your employees safe, and giving them a clear path to follow.

Let me reiterate that I realize that what I propose a lot of times takes effort, time, work, and money to implement. I know it may be a long process to make it happen and there may be some bumps along the way.

But don't give up; following through and spending the time, effort, and money is well worth the results.

One company I work with went from an average of 80 percent click ratio with fewer than 10 percent reporting to a 9 percent click ratio with an average of 64 percent reporting. That same company has seen a consistent 70 percent reduction in the number of malware incidents due to the policies now in place.

Was it an overnight turnaround? Nope. Those results took a few years, but how worth it do you think it was? It was only through consistent phishing, regular education, and hard work that we got those numbers.

As a program starts working, we have seen some companies get too caught up in the numbers. Remember, the main purpose for having a phishing program is to educate on the threat of phishing and show how the program is working in your population. Sometimes the statistics can entice you to focus too much on the numbers and not the people or the goal.

We have, unfortunately, witnessed companies get so into the statistics they forget about the people and want to just show the numbers. Stick to the program and remember that your goal is to increase the number of reporters and decrease the number of clickers. Doing this may take time, but "fudging" the numbers won't make your people learn any faster.

The final question is really this: How do you choose the type of SaaS (Software as a Service) or software to run? That topic is explored in Chapter 7.

The Professional Phisher's Tackle Bag

"Technology is just a tool."
—Bill Gates

I remember the first time my grandpa took me deep sea fishing. I was about five or six years old. We went on this large boat that headed out into the ocean. The farther we got from shore, the less land I could see. Was I scared? Not at all—but why not? My grandpa tied a large rope around my waist and then tied the other end to the railing of the boat. I can remember him saying, "At least if you fall over we can reel in a big shark!"

We got out to our designated area, and the boat hands pulled out these giant rods. The reels were bigger than me, and the lines had giant hooks at the end. The boat hands attached a giant shrimp to the hook and then let the line down into the water before handing me a rod. My tiny little hands could barely hold the rod, let alone reel anything in. When the boat hands saw my struggle, they handed me a tiny "Tony the Tiger" fishing pole. I felt like the big man on campus, but I was never going to catch anything with that rod.

Why? It was the wrong tool for the job. The first rod was the right tool, but I didn't have the strength or skill to wield it. And herein lies the lesson that composes this chapter.

Up to now we have discussed all the psychology behind phishing, the rationale to create a great program, and the logic behind deciding how to proceed while avoiding common pitfalls. The last piece of the puzzle is the tools.

Not just the tools, though. It would be easy to just throw at you a list of every tool out there and say, "Have fun!" Instead I want to give you an overview of the tools from a professional phisher's point of view.

I decided to give you an overview of every tool *that I have personally used*. This chapter explains what the tool is, whether it is free or commercial, the pros and cons of the tool, and what I thought about the tool. At the end of the chapter I provide a side-by-side comparison of all these tools.

But wait . . . there's more. The chapter concludes with a discussion of Software as a Service (SaaS) versus Managed Services versus do-it-yourself to help you to understand where you fit best.

My goal is not to bias you one way or the other but to provide an honest appraisal of what I have used over the last five or so years as I have professionally phished millions of people. To accomplish this goal while being as unbiased as possible, I spoke to the makers of the top five commercial tools I have used and also the makers of the Social-Engineer Toolkit (SET) and PhishFrenzy, which are open source options. I asked them the following questions and said they could send me screenshots of the products:

- How would you describe your tool?
- What are the top pros of your tool?
- What are the top cons of your tool?

The companies had the choice to respond to one, some, all, or none of the questions. The questions they responded to are part of this chapter. (I edited the responses to remove any sales pitches.) At the end of each section I included my personal notes, which are biased, of course, but my coverage of the products endeavors to answer these questions:

- What level of knowledge is needed to use the tool?
- What is the overall security of customer info?
- Are there any other challenges in using the tool (for example, time required to load recipient lists, ease of navigating the graphical user interface [GUI], ability to send multiple campaigns, ease of reporting)?
- What is the availability of tech support?

Let's get started.

Commercial Applications

This first section covers commercial applications, which are the packages that you must pay for. The following products represent what I view to be the leaders in the phishing software industry. Later I cover the available open source tools.

Rapid7 Metasploit Pro

Skilled penetration testers are hard to find, so it's important to use their time effectively. Rapid7 Metasploit Pro (`www.rapid7.com/products/ metasploit/editions-and-features.jsp`) helps prioritize and demonstrate risk through closed-loop vulnerability validation, and it measures security awareness through simulated phishing e-mails. Integration with Rapid7 NeXpose (`www.rapid7.com/products/nexpose/`) validates vulnerabilities in your environment, demonstrates risk, and prioritizes action plans. End-to-end phishing campaigns allow you to safely test user behavior with analytics to tell you who fell for the bait. Plus, you can view campaign results in Rapid7 UserInsight (`www.rapid7.com/ products/user-insight/`) for a more complete view of user risk.

Pros

- With Rapid7 you can assess both security awareness of users and optionally the effectiveness of security controls through penetration testing techniques—for example, exploitation and Java payloads.

- Rapid7 is an all-round offensive security tool that goes beyond phishing. It also covers exploitation, credentials, and web app testing.

- It's an on-premise application that ensures privacy of your findings inside your own network.

- Rapid7 integrates with UserInsight to provide an overview of user risk beyond phishing.

- You need one license for unlimited users and phishing campaigns.

Cons

- The on-premise product requires hosting and maintenance on your own network.

- Phishing templates are very basic.

- The built-in training modules are very basic phishing training (but it can be integrated with a third-party training solution).

- Exploitation may be too intrusive for some customers. You can switch it off if you want.

Screenshots

Figures 7-1 and 7-2 show screenshots from Rapid7 Metasploit Pro.

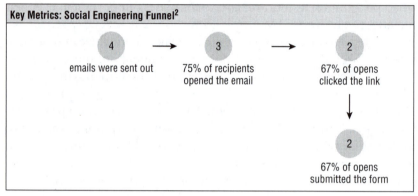

Figure 7-1: Rapid7 Metasploit Pro statistics page

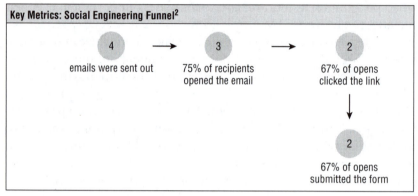

Figure 7-2: Rapid7 Metasploit Pro campaign tracker

My Thoughts

This is my assessment of Metasploit Pro:

- What level of knowledge was needed to use the tool?

  Setting up campaigns in Metasploit Pro was not difficult. I felt it was intuitive and didn't require any special level of software knowledge. As with all software, the learning curve is in the GUI, and some things were not labeled the way I was accustomed to, but overall I found it moderately easy to use.

  I wouldn't say that Metasploit Pro is made for novices, but you don't need to be an engineer to work with it. There were a few questions I had on some simple matters, such as how to see results or set up spoofed e-mails, but with some good documentation and a few short training sessions I was on my way with little problem.

- What is the overall security of customer info?

  Because Metasploit Pro is self-hosted, the security is largely dependent on your setup. If you put the software on a public-facing server with no security, then it is more likely to be compromised. We did not run security audits on the software itself to determine the level of internal security, but the system is password protected and does seem to use a good level of security with regard to protecting customer data. The bottom line is this: Because Metasploit Pro is a self-hosted tool, it is up to you to make it secure.

- Are there any other challenges in using the tool?

  The GUI seemed intuitive for the most part, but I had some confusion on how to set up e-mail servers and sending times. The version I used did not allow me to schedule e-mails to be sent, and I could not send more than one campaign at a time. Reporting was available, and I could export the data, which helped me create custom reports for our clients.

- What is the availability of tech support?

The team I was assigned was quick to answer questions and helped walk me through the parts I was confused about.

ThreatSim

ThreatSim (http://threatsim.com/) enables organizations to assess and reduce risk associated with end-user behavior. ThreatSim is a security awareness platform that educates employees on how to identify potential threats and how to make security-minded decisions. ThreatSim's original product enables organizations to send simulated phishing attacks against end users and provides immediate training to those who fall prey to the phish. Newer products include additional scenario-based training focused on common situations in which employees are faced with a decision that affects security. The ThreatScore user risk management product rates employees based on their historical behavior, security knowledge, technical profile, and job characteristics by providing actionable data that security managers can use to reduce risk posed by their end users. ThreatSim is offered in a SaaS model and is sold as an annual subscription based on the number of end users.

Pros

- **Extensive customization options:** ThreatSim provides users with options to customize phishing and training messages. Phishing message customization includes e-mail sender name, address, landing domain, and a full editor for the message content, including the ability to cut and paste real-world phishing messages into the editor for your campaigns. ThreatSim's data-entry campaigns are realistic when you use the company's website scrapping feature to create simulated malicious landing pages. Each of the training messages are 100 percent customizable, including the content, graphics, and layouts, which enables customers to create messages that meet their specific requirements.

- **Vulnerability detection:** ThreatSim inspects the target's browser to identify out-of-date software (such as Java, Adobe, and Flash) that increases the target's susceptibility to malware infections initiated by the phishing attack.

- **Advanced phishing simulation features:** ThreatSim provides several features for advanced phishing simulations, including but not limited to the ability to stagger the delivery of phishing messages over a period of time to better simulate real-world phishing attacks, dynamic list creation based on how often targets are "repeat offenders," and the ability to assign a risk rating to each target based on that person's historical performance and technical profile.

- **Ease of use:** ThreatSim's interface (see Figure 7-3) provides an efficient means to create campaigns and review results. ThreatSim's e-mail list management provides a simple two-step update process that removes employees no longer with the organization and adds new hires. ThreatSim enables a full data export for customers who need the ability to perform advanced analytics.

- **Multi-language support:** Global organizations increasingly are the targets of phishing attacks and require the ability to localize content for more effective phishing training, so ThreatSim includes extensive language support. Content is translated into 14 languages, with new languages added based on customer need.

Cons

There's just one main con with ThreatSim: information overload. The amount of data that ThreatSim gives can be daunting to some users.

Screenshots

Figures 7-3 through 7-7 show screenshots from ThreatSim.

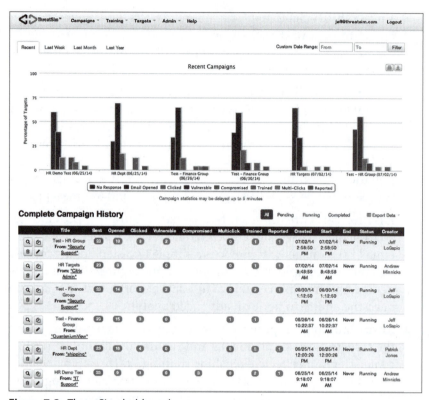

Figure 7-3: ThreatSim dashboard

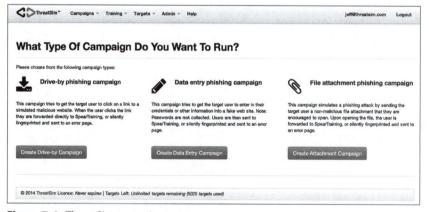

Figure 7-4: ThreatSim campaign setup

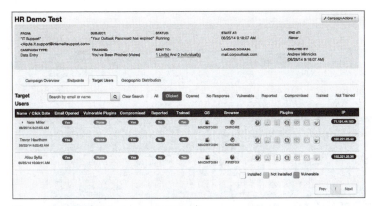

Figure 7-5: ThreatSim campaign results

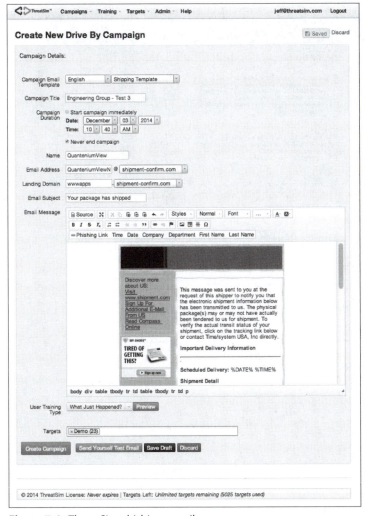

Figure 7-6: ThreatSim phishing e-mail

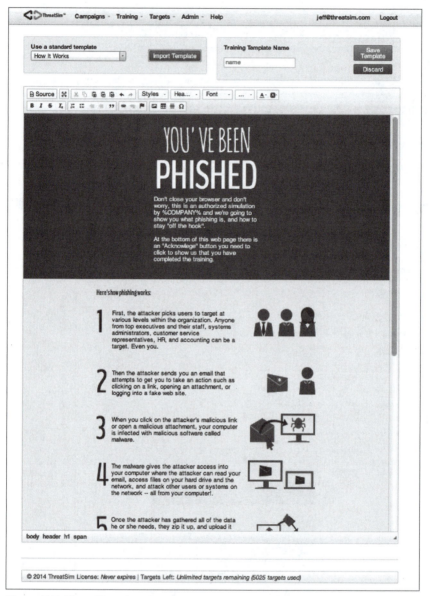

Figure 7-7: ThreatSim education page

My Thoughts

This is my assessment of ThreatSim:

- What level of knowledge was needed to use the tool?

  ThreatSim was made to be easy to use. It is certainly made for the novice-level user, but it also has robust features. I found it very easy to set up an e-mail for phishing. Importing lists for users and scheduling the sending was also very intuitive. The reporting was not as robust as I would have liked, and I ended up exporting the data to create my own report. The ThreatSim team is constantly improving and enhancing the product, and overall it was a very easy tool to use.

  In addition, there are some newer features that have made ThreatSim easier to use. My favorite of these is dynamic list generation. This means I can add criteria to my list and then create a list of all the employees who meet those criteria. For example, I can set the criterion as "Language Spoken" and then create a list of all Spanish-speaking folks at my client and phish only those people with a Spanish-language e-mail.

  Some other features are customizable training videos and some enhanced training tools for those users who click the phish.

- What is the overall security of customer info?

  ThreatSim is a hosted service and uses its own servers to host the databases. ThreatSim also uses Amazon Web Servers for load balancing. This may present issues depending on your needs. I had the opportunity to test ThreatSim in sending a phish of thousands of e-mails and it worked well. We did not perform security audits on the ThreatSim platform, so I cannot speak on the levels of software security. There is multistage authentication in the setup to ensure those who access the system are allowed to do so.

- Are there any other challenges in using the tool?

  There were no other challenges that are worth mentioning.

- What is the availability of tech support?

The team at ThreatSim was very responsive to problems. We had an issue with one large campaign, and the support team worked on it with us way past "normal" hours to resolve the issue.

PhishMe

PhishMe (http://phishme.com/) is an SaaS solution that utilizes immersive education methods to train employees to identify and avoid phishing attacks. With PhishMe, an organization's employees are immersed in a real-world phishing experience. In addition, employees are empowered to report suspicious phishing attempts using PhishMe Reporter (http://phishme.com/product-services/reporter/), which provides a source of real-time threat intelligence to security operations and incident response teams. The advanced reporting capability tracks user and group behavior for individual scenarios and cumulative response trends over time. Using the reporting you can provide demonstrable evidence of your organization's areas of susceptibility and security behavior management progress.

Pros

- **Programmatic approach:** PhishMe does not provide a tool for one-off assessments. Instead it helps organizations build a sustainable program, customized to their culture and business requirements.

- **Realistic scenarios and content:** PhishMe is continually updating content to address the latest phishing trends, keep content realistic, and inform an organization's infosec staff of the latest threats.

- **Proactive reporting:** PhishMe's patented e-mail plug-in, PhishMe Reporter, enables users to proactively report suspicious e-mail activity to security operations or incident response in a standardized contextual format. User reporting provides another feed of data for early detection of phishing attacks and acts as another measure of program efficacy.

- **Benchmarking:** Organizations can use structured exercises to anonymously compare their results with those of other PhishMe customers. In addition, an organization can compare its results with those of industry peers.

- **Enterprise-grade platform:** The PhishMe SaaS solution operates on dedicated infrastructure in secure hosting facilities. The U.S. instance is on dedicated systems located in a SOC 3–certified facility. The European instance meets ISO 9001 and 27001 standards to address European Union or other jurisdictional privacy regulations.

Cons

PhishMe declined to offer a list of cons for the product.

Screenshots

Figures 7-8 through 7-10 show screenshots from PhishMe.

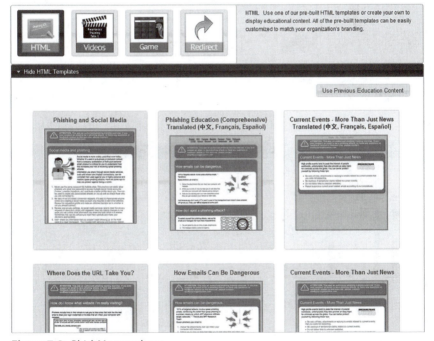

Figure 7-8: PhishMe templates

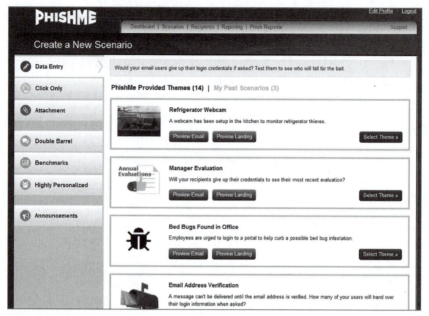

Figure 7-9: PhishMe scenarios

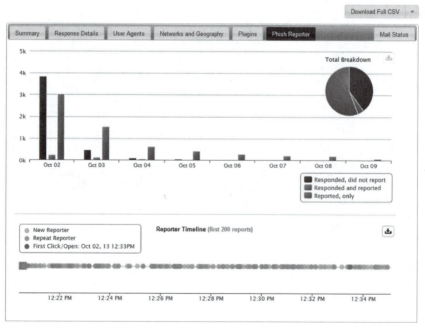

Figure 7-10: PhishMe Reporter

My Thoughts

This is my assessment of PhishMe:

- What level of knowledge was needed to use the tool?

  PhishMe was made to be easy to use. It was developed with the beginner or novice in mind. It is easy to set up campaigns. The interface for organizing lists and scheduling campaigns is intuitive.

  It was simple to upload lists, and I easily found the reporting data without having much knowledge of the software. The layout and design were made for a novice to come in and be able to quickly get up to speed.

- What is the overall security of customer info?

  As with the previously described software, I did not perform security audits on the PhishMe platform to speak on the levels of security. PhishMe is compliant with many security protocols and has multistaged authentication. In addition, the company does not use Amazon Web Servers to load balance—it has its own set of servers—so none of your data is ever running off any servers except PhishMe's.

- Are there any other challenges in using the tool?

  There were some limitations for us in using PhishMe. Although the platform is easy to use, I felt it lacked some of the robust features I saw in other platforms, such as custom reporting. In addition, change requests were very slow in being addressed.

- What is the availability of tech support?

  The PhishMe tech support teams are very competent but very slow. My requests generally would be not be answered in the same day, and in one case a project was actually delayed due to slow response times and lack of communication from the tech support teams.

Wombat PhishGuru

With Wombat Security's PhishGuru (`http://www.wombatsecurity.com/solutions/anti-phishing-training-suite`) mock attack phishing service, you can assess your employees' vulnerability to attack and motivate them to take training by sending them mock phishing e-mails. When an employee falls for a mock attack, it creates a unique "teachable moment."

Employees are immediately presented with a 10-second message that explains what happened and how to avoid similar attacks in the future.

Falling for the mock attack awakens employees to their vulnerability and motivates them to take follow-up interactive training. PhishGuru includes an auto-enrollment feature that sends a training assignment e-mail immediately after an employee falls for a mock attack.

Pros

- Automation features improve the effectiveness of mock phishing attacks and lead to significant reduction in successful phishing attacks from the wild.

- The auto-enroll feature integrates PhishGuru and its Security Education Platform and allows you to automatically assign follow-up in-depth training to users who have fallen for a simulated phishing attack.

- You can select the days of the week and hours of a day that mock phishing e-mails can be sent randomly to your list of end users. Spreading out the e-mail distribution times and randomizing the recipients reduces the chances that employees can figure out they are being targets of mock attacks.

- The phishing e-mail content is embedded in the teachable moment the employee receives after she falls for a mock phishing attack. This ensures the employee understands what she should have seen in the e-mail to clue her in on the phishing attack.

- You can customize the defined fields for intelligent reporting of the results.

- New phishing templates are added every month to mimic attacks from the wild.

Cons

PhishGuru does not supply phishing templates with other company's brands without permission from the company.

Screenshots

Figures 7-11 through 7-13 show screenshots from PhishGuru.

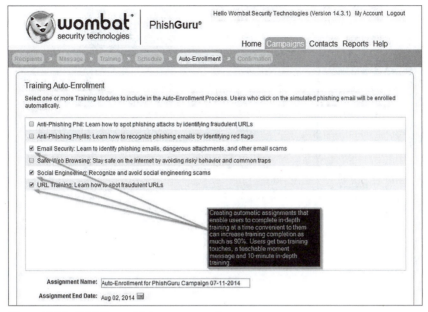

Figure 7-11: PhishGuru training auto-enrollment

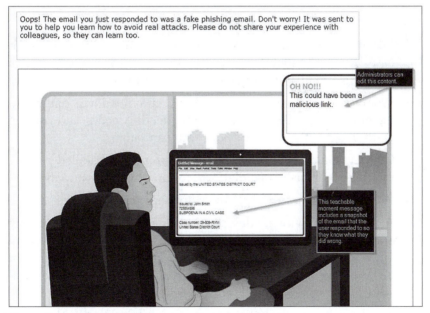

Figure 7-12: PhishGuru training page

Figure 7-13: PhishGuru SMS testing landing page

My Thoughts

This is my assessment of PhishGuru:

- ▪ What level of knowledge was needed to use the tool?

  Like much of the other software in this list, PhishGuru is made for ease of use. The tool is pretty straightforward when setting up a phishing e-mail and campaign and importing lists.

  Wombat Security has spent considerable time on developing training modules for all sorts of social-engineering tactics, and you can easily include those modules in your campaigns.

  Overall, you do not need to be a programmer or a skilled phisher to utilize the PhishGuru platform to run phishing campaigns.

- ▪ What is the overall security of customer info?

  As with the previously described tools, I did not do any security audits for platform security, but PhishGuru does use multistage authentication for logging in, and it allows for segregation of instances for customers. While I used it, I did not find that it possessed any major flaws. It ran very smoothly and easily.

- ▪ Are there any other challenges in using the tool?

  There were no other major challenges in the tool.

- ▪ What is the availability of tech support?

Wombat Security has tech support. My personal experience with Wombat Security's tech support was very positive. The team was responsive to suggestions and ideas and quick to react. I found the team be very professional, easy to work with, and interested in the customer.

PhishLine

PhishLine (www.phishline.com/) is an enterprise SaaS solution that provides real-world social-engineering and phishing simulations along with online security awareness training, risk-based surveys, and detailed, risk-based reporting and metrics.

Pros

- **Multi-vector attack simulations:** PhishLine provides the ability to test and measure more than just traditional link-based e-mail phishing simulations. The solution provides testing and measurement capabilities that include portable media, text, voice, simulated portal pages, smart attachments, and a range of customization capabilities that allow security professionals to test and measure real-world security threats with precision.

- **Reporting and metrics:** PhishLine collects a lot of actionable data, and the software makes it easy to perform analytics at a level historically reserved for dedicated analytics platforms. PhishLine's metrics and reporting capabilities go beyond summary reporting to provide visibility into the people, process, and technology layers of social-engineering and phishing threats. PhishLine delivers levels of custom reporting and meaningful metrics that are immediately actionable.

- **Commitment to customer service:** PhishLine's development and support structure is composed of security professionals. This is an important fact when it comes to the type of software that is generally supported just by developers. The support team gets not only the software but the intricacies of phishing and security threats.

- **Risk-based integration with real-world security programs:** Customers can use PhishLine to deliver targeted online security awareness training, conduct risk-based surveys, and incorporate key metrics and discoveries from the solution into their overall security and risk program.

Cons

For those first starting out, the depth of the interface and customization capabilities might seem complex compared to that of other tools.

Screenshots

Figures 7-14 through 7-16 show screenshots from PhishLine.

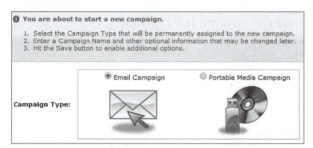

Figure 7-14: PhishLine campaign starter

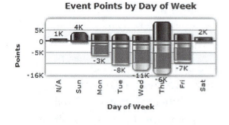

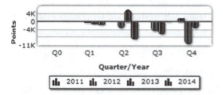

Figure 7-15: PhishLine tracking screens

Figure 7-16: PhishLine outlined plan for phishing simulations

My Thoughts

This is my assessment of PhishLine:

- What level of knowledge was needed to use the tool?

  PhishLine boasts the most robust set of features out of all the tools I used. PhishLine's interface might not be as geared toward the novice as the other products', but it is not any more difficult to determine how to set up phishing e-mails, launch campaigns, and import lists.

  The true power of PhishLine is in the reporting. The software captures literally all the data required that anyone—from a novice to a complete data nut—could want. Reporting on that data might require a few lessons from PhishLine's capable trainers and support staff, but after you learn how to find what you're looking for, you will be amazed.

  PhishLine has a very in-depth custom reporting engine that can enable you to display any subset of data from any number of campaigns. One of my favorite features is how PhishLine ties incident response into its reporting, which allows the company to manage incident response by using mail-forwarding features already built into all mail clients. You can then track, catalog, and report who responds appropriately so you can clearly see who "passed."

  In the end, PhishLine is the most complex of all the GUIs from the commercial options, but it also is one of the most powerful.

- What is the overall security of customer info?

  Besides PhishMe, PhishLine is the only other hosted tool on the list that does not use Amazon Web Servers as a load balancer. I did not run security audits, but the fact that all of the load balancing and the platform are run from PhishLine's own servers does add a layer of security.

  Through my experience with working with PhishLine on a few secure projects, I can attest that the team sets up very secure servers for the handling of customer data and allows for the managing of separate instances for each customer.

- Are there any other challenges in using the tool?

  The only challenge in using PhishLine is the complexity of the interface. I needed a few training sessions to get up to speed with doing some things that might have been intuitive if I had been using some of the other systems.

- What is the availability of tech support?

  At the risk of sounding like an infomercial, I have to say that the tech support people at PhishLine are outstanding. I have literally seen them work until all hours of the night to help me fix a problem for a customer even though the problem wasn't the fault of PhishLine. They work tirelessly at improving the product, and without a doubt, they love to be told where they can improve. In my experience, they take the feedback and make improvements at lightning speed.

Open Source Applications

This short section covers two of the most widely used and well-known open source toolkits for social engineering: SET (Social-Engineer Toolkit) and Phishing Frenzy.

SET: Social-Engineer Toolkit

SET (`https://www.trustedsec.com/social-engineer-toolkit/`) provides a mechanism for assessors to test the effectiveness of their education and awareness program. SET, created by David Kennedy, is a technical tool that attempts to circumvent many of the regular protection mechanisms (such as antivirus software, application whitelisting, and so on) to see if both technical controls and user awareness can stop attacks. SET was derived from the need of the information security community to be able to test itself before actual hackers do. The most common methods of exploitation are through social engineering and phishing; SET uses these techniques to identify gaps in education and awareness programs.

SET gives organizations the ability to craft believable phishing e-mails where the end user has no idea that a possible phish is occurring. SET combines the latest technological attacks with the ability to quickly set up a malicious website without a lot of sophistication needed. SET makes it easy for organizations to test their security where it's most important—at the end user.

Pros

SET has a nice list of pros, which include the following:

- Ability to test how effectively users respond to targeted attacks that would be traditionally seen in the wild

- Easy and effective ways for penetration testers to create believable and realistic pretexts to attack an organization and compromise them

- Ability to track which users clicked e-mails and the ratio of how many people fell for the suspected attack

- Realistic scenarios that circumvent some of today's top preventative technologies

- Ability to gauge how well an organization can withstand an attack

Cons

- Some organizations have a hard time using open source tools.

- You cannot schedule e-mails.

- There is no GUI; SET is driven through the command line.

- The attacks require research of the targets in order to perform, as SET is more of a spear phishing platform.

Screenshots

Figures 7-17 through 7-19 show screenshots from SET.

```
set:payloads> Enter the number for the payload [meterpreter_revers
tcp]:
[*] Prepping pyInjector for delivery..
[*] Prepping website for pyInjector shellcode injection..
[*] Base64 encoding shellcode and prepping for delivery..
[*] Multi/Pyinjection was specified. Overriding config options.
[*] Generating x86-based powershell injection code...
[*] Finished generating powershell injection bypass.
[*] Encoded to bypass execution restriction policy...
[*] Apache appears to be running, moving files into Apache's home

*************************************************************
Web Server Launched. Welcome to the SET Web Attack.
*************************************************************

[--] Tested on Windows, Linux, and OSX [--]
[--] Apache web server is currently in use for performance. [--]
[*] Moving payload into cloned website.
[*] The site has been moved. SET Web Server is now listening..
[-] Launching MSF Listener...
[-] This may take a few to load MSF...
```

Figure 7-17: SET menu structure

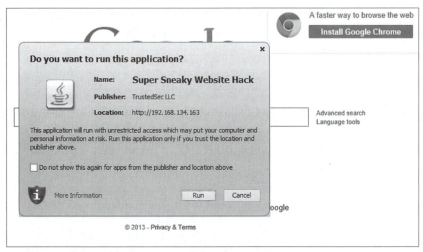

Figure 7-18: SET spoofed certs and web pages

```
msf exploit(handler) > [*] Meterpreter session 1 opened (192.168.13
4.163:443 -> 192.168.134.159:50921) at 2014-11-24 14:28:42 -0500

msf exploit(handler) > sessions -i 1
[*] Starting interaction with 1...

meterpreter > shell
Process 3696 created.
Channel 1 created.
Microsoft Windows [Version 6.3.9600]
(c) 2013 Microsoft Corporation. All rights reserved.

C:\Users\davek_000\Desktop>
```

Figure 7-19: SET getting a shell

My Thoughts

This is my assessment of SET:

- What level of knowledge was needed to use the tool?

  SET is powerful and has a ton of features. You work with it through the command line, so although it is heavily menu driven, you need to be comfortable using command-line tools and loading Python scripts.

  With that being said, Dave has created a menu-driven tool that is easy to learn.

- What is the overall security of customer info?

  This tool is hosted on your servers and your hardware, so security is really up to you and how you set it up.

- Are there any other challenges in using the tool?

  I have used SET on many projects—usually smaller phishing campaigns. Using it with a very large client that has thousands of e-mail addresses would require quite a lot of work. SET is a tool that assists the social-engineer penetration tester, but I'm not sure it's suited for monthly phishing programs.

- What is the availability of tech support?

  Dave does a great job of answering questions very quickly, but, as with any open source tool, it is essential that you first try to work through problems, read the documentation, and search the web for answers.

Phishing Frenzy

Phishing Frenzy (`www.phishingfrenzy.com/`) is an open source Linux-based Ruby on Rails application that is leveraged by penetration testers to manage e-mail phishing campaigns.

Pros

Phishing Frenzy offers the following:

- A truly flexible framework
- Ability to easily share templates and scenarios with others who use Phishing Frenzy
- Lots of features, such as real-time campaign tracking, ability to run multiple campaigns at once, and much more
- Open source, so you can make additions if you want

Cons

- Phishing Frenzy works only on the Linux operating system.
- Creating templates can be cumbersome.
- There is a slight learning curve.
- You cannot schedule e-mails.

Screenshots

Figures 7-20 through 7-22 show screenshots from Phishing Frenzy.

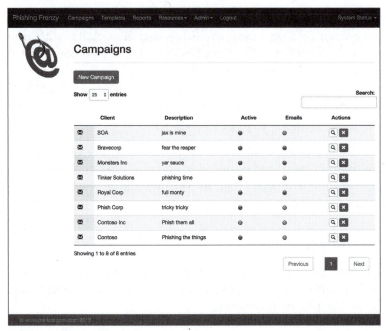

Figure 7-20: Phishing Frenzy campaign menu

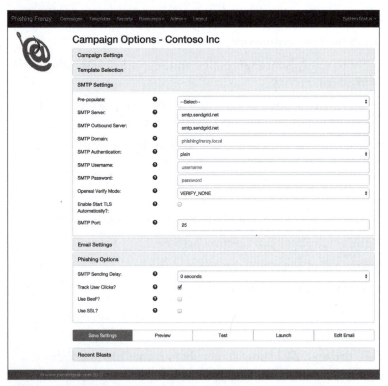

Figure 7-21: Phishing Frenzy campaign options

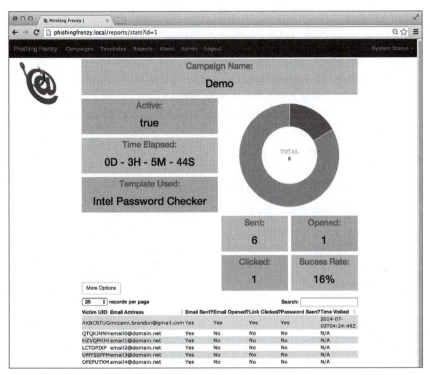

Figure 7-22: Phishing Frenzy campaign stats

My Thoughts

This is my assessment of Phishing Frenzy:

■ What level of knowledge was needed to use the tool?

Phishing Frenzy is a very nice open source tool. The menus are easy to understand, the layout makes sense, and I don't think using the tool requires a very high level of knowledge. My main concern is in the way phishing e-mails are created. There is no WYSIWYG (what you see is what you get) platform to write e-mails within Phishing Frenzy. Instead you have to use an HTML editor on your local machine, upload the .html file to the server, and assign it to the template for a phishing e-mail. That one issue makes me give it an out-of-novice-range user rating.

■ What is the overall security of customer info?

This tool is hosted on your servers and your hardware, so security really depends on you and how you set it up.

■ Are there any other challenges in using the tool?

Besides the difficulty in setting up the e-mails, Phishing Frenzy is very easy to use and understand. Reporting is not robust, but you can export data to make more robust reports. For an open source tool, it is a good option.

I have sent campaigns that consisted of a few hundred e-mails from Phishing Frenzy. In the latest campaigns in which I used the tool, I experienced no problems with it.

■ What is the availability of tech support?

This is not what the developer does for a living, so the answers you get are actually quite fast considering he has a day job. He is responsive in helping with the setup of the server and also fixing any bugs found.

Comparison Chart

This chapter includes a lot of information—so much information that even though I have used all these tools I had a hard time keeping all the details straight. I decided what might help is a handy chart that outlines the features with a quick reference to tell you what features exist and don't exist in each tool.

Here's a legend for the chart in Figure 7-23:

Y = Yes, the feature exists in this tool.

N = No, the feature does not exist in this tool.

NA = Not applicable; this feature doesn't apply at all to this tool.

* or = A footnote in the chart gives more information about that particular answer feature.

FEATURE	RAPID7 COMM	THREATSIM COMM	PHISHME COMM	WOMBAT COMM	PHISHLINE COMM	SET O-S	PHISHING FRENZY O-S
Allow for scheduled start times for campaigns?	Y	Y	Y	Y	Y	N	N
Allow for scheduled times to stop the campaign?	Y	Y	Y	Y	Y	N	N
Allow for the use of logos from vendors to simulate phishing e-mails?	Y	Y	Y*	N	Y	Y	Y
Allow for export of all data?	N	Y	Y	Y	Y	Y	Y
Handle incident response or reporting?	N	Y	Y	N	Y	N	N
If yes, does it have stats for who reported/clicked, reported/no click?	NA	Y	Y	NA	Y	NA	NA
Allow for SMSing tests?	N	N	Y	Y	Y	Y	N
Allow for USB/media creation tests?	Y	Y	Y	Y	Y	Y	Y
Allow for spoofing of e-mail addresses?	N	Y	Y	Y	Y	Y	NA
Multistaged authentication?	NA	Y	Y	Y	Y	NA	Y*
Use Amazon Web Servers for load balancing?	NA	Y	N	Y	N	NA	N
Have segregated instances for each customer?	Y	Y	Y#	Y	Y	NA	Y
Allow for importing from XLS, CSV?	Y	Y	Y	Y	Y	N	Y
Has live tech support?	Y	Y	Y	Y	Y	N	N
Ability to run multiple simultaneous campaigns?	N	Y	Y	Y	Y	N	Y
Limitations on numbers of e-mails sent in one campaign?	N	N	N	N	N	N	
			* Only w/ permission # Upon request				* Depends on your setup

Figure 7-23: Software comparison chart

Managed or Not

There's one last avenue I need to talk about, even though it might seem self-serving; it's still an important option for you to consider: having someone manage your program.

All the software and tools I mentioned in this chapter have to be run by someone, so do you want someone in-house to run it for you or do you want a company like mine to run your program for you?

This is a question that I cannot answer for you, but I can at least give you some questions and thoughts to ponder as you make the decision:

- Will the phishing program be the only job that your in-house person has to manage, or will that person have to fit it in with his other work? As you can see from the previous chapters, running a program is a full-time job.

- Remember that for each month you want to send a phish, you need to update the user lists, make sure your e-mails are approved, and write a professional report.

- Does your in-house person or outside vendor have experience in writing, reviewing, and rating phishing e-mails?

- Does your in-house person or outside vendor have experience in social-engineering attacks as a pentester—a skill that can help him with pretexts?

- How much time per month do you want to devote to this program? This question can help you determine whether you need new staff, an outside vendor, or an in-house team to manage the program.

The decision you make doesn't have to last a lifetime. Right now I work with a handful of companies that started their phishing programs using in-house staff who worked with one of the tools described in this chapter. After running the program for many months, the companies realized they needed help to manage it and came to us to help them.

Another client that we still do pentesting for ran its own program for a year and then decided to try to manage the phishing program in-house. And the client is doing a great job at it!

Whatever option you pick, you can switch it up later if you decide it works better for you on the flipside. Or you may find you love the decision you made and keep it that way. What is most important is that—one way or another—you are educating your staff on the dangers of phishing.

Summary

This chapter was designed to help you put together the information from the previous six chapters and find a tool to help you implement the plan you have in mind. Does that mean using an open source or commercial product? Does that mean using a tool that has more robust features or more novice-oriented features? Those are questions that you need to answer for yourself—or you can contact a vendor who can help you assess your needs.

As I stated earlier, what is truly important is that now you are thinking about how to implement a phishing program in your organization. Choosing a tool is an important part of this decision. Imagine you decide to build a birdhouse, but the only tool you grab is a ruler. You would get nowhere fast, and you would be frustrated and give up.

The right tool that fits your needs and fits your program eliminates your frustration, helps you get the program moving faster, and helps you focus on the education rather than the actual process. I truly hope this chapter helped you with that choice.

CHAPTER

8

Phish Like a Boss

"I will miss our conversations."
—Nathan Algren,
The Last Samurai

In the short time that it took Chris and me to write this book, the world has moved on. There have been a number of additional high-profile breaches reported, including eBay, The Home Depot, Sony, Chick-fil-A, and JPMorgan Chase & Co. I think it's safe to say that we haven't begun to see all of the fallout that will surely come in the form of stolen credit cards or identities or further attempts to perpetrate theft or infiltration through phishing.

The most recent report published from the Anti-Phishing Working Group (APWG), released August 29, 2014,[1] reveals that the second quarter of 2014 had the second highest number of unique phishing websites reported—128,378. In addition, the number of unique phish reported in this same time frame was 171,801. These are just the numbers reported to the APWG, so I don't think it's a leap of logic to assume that this is only a fraction of phish and malicious websites circulating in the wild. The trend has been a continual increase over the last decade that the APWG has been reporting.

What's worse, phishers are becoming quicker, smarter, and more adaptive. In a recent study[2] on manual account hijacking conducted by Google and the University of California, San Diego, it was determined that an attacker attempted to access 20 percent of accounts with harvested credentials within 30 minutes and 50 percent within 7 hours. In addition, attackers spent an average of 3 minutes searching accounts to determine their value based on e-mails containing information such as financial data or other account credentials. Finally, they found that a contact of a compromised account was 36 times more likely to receive a phishing e-mail, indicating that phishers use a victim's friends and associates to launch additional attacks.

Any way you look at it, phishing is going to continue to be a problem for people and organizations in the foreseeable future. The only real solution is staying educated and aware in all of your online activities.

Phishing the Deep End

It was not easy for us to try to come up with a final chapter that didn't just rehash all we said in the previous seven. Michele and I talked about how we would want to conclude this book for you, and we came up with a short list of reminders and topics that we think summarizes the concepts we've presented and what we hope you take away from this book.

Understand What You're Dealing With

Phishing is not a recreational pastime; it's real business for bad guys. One report estimated that the loss to phishing in 2013 was over $5.9 billion.[3] Like any business, phishing continues to evolve and adapt to maintain its profitability. Although the Nigerian 419 scams are still alive and very well, there is a consistent trend toward phish that are more realistic and don't include the easy identifiers that we're accustomed to relying on as we try to spot phish.

In addition, phishers know what motivates people and have no issues using sensitive topics and human tragedy to get you to click.

Increases in Phishing: What Do They Mean for You?

Unfortunately, advanced phishing means having to think a little more about the e-mails you receive. Here are some simple rules I give to my non-tech friends and family:

- If you're at home and you don't know who sent the e-mail, don't open it; just delete it. If you are at your place of work, report it to the proper internal agency that handles phishing.
- If the e-mail comes from someone you know, think critically before clicking any attachments or links. Do the contents of the e-mail

match the behavior you expect from that person? If the sender is making a request, does it make sense? If there's any doubt about whether the e-mail really came from that individual, contact her through alternate means.

- If the e-mail comes from an entity that you interact with online (for example, a bank or social media), either call or go to the website in your browser rather than click the link provided in the e-mail. *Never* provide credentials or personal information through e-mail. The five extra seconds you spend on communicating your personal information via a known good method can save you your identity.

Now, following these guidelines may mean you might not get an update from a friend or will miss out on an online deal. But the alternatives are consequences that range from a compromised computer all the way to stolen identity. If you have a good understanding of the scale of the phishing problem and potential outcomes, a little critical thinking now can go a long way toward saving a lot of grief later.

As I was writing this chapter, I had a meeting at a company where a user had clicked on a phish and downloaded some ransomware via e-mail. The ransomware encrypted the user's whole drive and also the entire network and connected drives. The technique the hackers used to create the application was solid cryptography, and there were no implementation flaws for breaking it. This means the user has to either pay the ransom or lose the data (if it's not properly backed up). Would not a few more seconds of critical thinking and having to open a browser instead of clicking the attachment been worth preventing that loss?

Increase in Phishing: What Do They Mean for the Information Security Pros?

Unfortunately, the security professional's job just gets bigger and bigger. We find only a few organizations are willing to spend the money on consultants or larger teams, so the security pros in these companies have to be jacks-of-all-trades. Clearly, the best option is a phishing education and testing program facilitated by people who understand the ins and outs of the trade. But if you don't have that, there are still things you can do:

- Stay as current as you can on popular phish and methodologies by visiting sites like `www.apwg.org` and `www.social-engineer.com`. If you still think phishing is a low-threat vector perpetrated by uneducated thugs, it might be wise to update your knowledge. Hopefully this book helped you a little bit in establishing some basic knowledge.

■ Build phishing and general social-engineering education into your security awareness program. It probably won't cover everything at once, but just starting a conversation to alert your employees is better than hoping the problem goes away.

After you understand the nature and scope of phishing, the ultimate goal is to develop a coherent program that regularly tests and educates your organization on identifying and properly responding to phish in the wild.

Set Realistic Goals for Your Organization

In an ideal world, we'd catch all the bad e-mails coming in and conduct our daily business without interruption. Because that's never the case, what can you realistically accomplish? Goal-setting is a fundamental part of having a phishing program. If you don't know what you're shooting for, you won't know when you've arrived or how to correct your course along the way.

Goal-setting is highly dependent on your organization's culture and leadership. Do you have a company that constantly experiences high turnover? Are you lucky enough to work for a company where good communication is the norm? Are you in an environment with highly reactive management? Do you have any idea of where your organization currently sits with respect to phishing awareness? There are many factors to consider when setting realistic goals, but here are a couple of things to ponder:

■ **Time frame:** How quickly do you expect to see change? Believing behaviors will shift in a few months is probably not realistic, even in very small companies. We have clients who have worked years to create awareness and improvement in their corporate culture. Phishing education is not a one-and-done kind of topic. Effective phishing programs don't end until the threat no longer exists. However, it is not unrealistic to start seeing some culture change in a few months; just know that the drastic changes generally take a bit longer.

■ **Metrics:** How will you measure change? If you don't start with a good understanding of your current status, you won't be able to measure meaningful improvement. If you choose to test only a portion of your population at a time, looking at month-to-month changes in click ratios is meaningless. Consider also other indicators of change, such as reporting behaviors and even more concrete measures, such as the detection rate of malware on your network (often introduced via phish).

Good goals are the foundation of an effective program.

Plan Your Program

There's a lot more to a coherent phishing-awareness program than just sending a random phish every month/quarter/year. You've set goals; how are you going to go about accomplishing them? Ask yourself the following questions:

- What phishing tool will we use, and why?
- How will we establish the corporate baseline?
- How often will we phish?
- How quickly will we advance the difficulty level?
- How will we report our numbers (simple click rate, reporting rate, other stats)?
- How do we want our employees to react to suspicious e-mails?
- What mechanisms do the employees have for reporting suspicious e-mails?
- What are the repercussions for "repeat offenders"?
- What are the repercussions for the folks who do well?
- How will we work all of this information into relevant education?

All of these factors should be considered in your program planning. The more time you spend up front, the smoother the program will run. Even hitches will be more predictable, and you'll at least have an idea of how to adjust accordingly.

Understand the Stats

We recently had a jubilant client come to us to report a click rate that fell by 50 percent from one month to the next. Fifty percent! That's really great, right? Well, maybe. Here's the problem: They had decided to test only a portion of the population each month with the goal of testing the entire company over the course of the year. There were no groups who received repeat testing over that time frame. What did a month-to-month reduction mean? Perhaps people were talking to fellow employees and getting the word around that the company was conducting phishing testing. Or maybe the second group happened to get a phish that was easier to detect. Or perhaps that second group happened to be more tech savvy than the first. There's no way to know the reason for the fall in click rate.

You need to understand what the numbers mean and don't mean. For a set of numbers to be statistically significant—that is, *the difference between groups is attributable to a manipulated variable as opposed to chance*—certain conditions have to exist. That's a problem for you stats guys to get into, and it's well beyond the scope of this book, but it's something you have to consider.

There are too many things that can affect the outcome. Chances are that if we asked the right questions, these groups might also be noticeably different in other meaningless ways, such as favorite types of music, IQ, and number of kids. See my point? So I would be very hesitant to say that a big difference from one month to the next is very significant. But if that trend continues month to month, then we can start to make some more positive conclusions, even without bringing in your resident statistician. The point we are trying to make is that if you are consistently hitting 80 percent click ratios and have hardly any reporting, and next month you get a 10 percent click ratio, before you rejoice and determine you can be done with phishing education, understand why that happened.

Was it that all your people were on vacation? Did the reporting ratio also go up? Was the phish something that more people paid attention to? What was the reason for the massive spike? If it is a one-off occurrence, then you will see the numbers change for the worse the next month. When you see continual improvement, then you can rejoice.

One final point: The context should also include the point of your program. We understand that *some* metrics are important to help you measure change over time and, frankly, to provide management with justification for the program, but keep in mind that your program should theoretically be about teaching your folks to recognize and deal with phish—not create pages and pages of metrics.

Respond Appropriately

By now we hope it's pretty clear that we're all about fixing security issues by creating a secure culture and educating your people—not getting rid of them. Good education has lots of benefits for both the employer and the employee. By creating smart and aware staff, you're teaching them good habits that will carry over to their personal lives as well. The only downside to a good security education program is that it *will* cost in terms of time, effort, and resources. Unfortunately, we've gotten past the point that spending on security is anything other than mandatory. The risks are too great to not make the investment. The good news, though, is that the benefits to your organization far outweigh the cost.

However, there are some people who just don't get it. Despite training and numerous warnings, these people still click every link they get through e-mail. They post on forums using work e-mail addresses. They make announcements on social media that detail internal workings of your company. Unfortunately, these people really do put your business at risk.

If you have a person in your organization who does these things and you've already tried multiple ways to educate this person, your choices become fairly limited. You can move the person to a different—and hopefully less damaging—part of your organization (think of Milton in the movie *Office Space*), or, as a last resort, you can dismiss them. The downside to letting the person go, of course, is that you will likely have to replace the individual and will need to conduct all security training from the ground up with the new employee.

NOTE One company we worked with tried something that worked quite well: The employees' performances in the phishing program were tied to their bonuses and reviews. The company actually has a metric that if the employees "passed" the training, their bonuses could be affected positively. That certainly motivated people to wake up and pay attention.

Here's one last thought about responding appropriately: Organizations expect their personnel to support them by using safe practices and making wise choices. But it's even more important that the reverse is also true: The organization must support its personnel by creating policies and procedures that encourage safe behavior and don't place people in the position of having to choose between courtesy and giving inappropriate information away. Here are some things to ask at the organizational level:

- Does our company have a policy about employee social media?
- Is there a procedure in place to verify the identity of both telephone and in-person callers?

- Is there a guideline regarding how internal information should be stored/shared?

- Do our employees have a safe and convenient way to report suspicious incidents?

Help your employees help you. And while you're at it, make sure your management and C-level execs are participating in the program. Although they may not like the idea of being phished, they likely hold critical information and most certainly need the practice.

Make the Choice: Build Inside or Outside

Recently, I had the chance to speak in front of a group of people who were very interested in phishing programs. One question that came up was about how much time it actually takes to run a program. Of course, I can't really say exactly how much time it takes, but the following outline gives you an idea of what is involved:

1. Making sure the phishing e-mail is realistic, current, and relevant and isn't psychologically damaging to your population.

2. Running that e-mail through the appropriate departments to get approval. This will involve edits and new iterations.

3. Ensuring the lists are updated—adding new hires and removing those who have left the company.

4. Preparing the proper educational landing page.

5. Loading the system you will use with the e-mail lists, phishing e-mail, and landing pages.

6. Scheduling and testing the sending of the e-mail.

7. Ensuring the e-mail is sent without any problems.

8. Collecting all data, which might include number of clicks, number of people who report the phish, and so on.

9. Writing the report and giving information in regard to positive or negative trends.

10. Repeating the process each month or quarter.

As you can see, this is not a part-time job, so assigning these tasks to an existing employee who already has a full-time job (and maybe has little to no skill in phishing or social engineering) can make this program ineffective and will hurt your chances of showing ROI (return on investment).

Maybe you can hire someone to help you run this program internally or you might have someone on staff that is perfect for the job. If so, that is an essential piece for a successful internal program.

But if you now realize that you don't have the staff, skill, or desire to run a phishing program internally and you want to search for a consultant to help you out, how should you get started? Of course, you can go to Google and search for "phishing consultants." You might get a few hits, and you certainly will find more than a handful of companies that will claim to have expertise in phishing, so how can you decide? One thing you can do is ask consultant candidates the following questions:

- How many phishing programs have you set up?
- How many phish have you sent?
- Do you use templates from the software or write your own?
- How much research has your company done into understanding why phishing works?
- Do you have statistics that show you've helped other companies reduce their clicks and increase their reporting?

TIP Remember: Anyone can write a phish that will get clicks. You are looking for someone to help you with positive change.

In addition to asking the preceding questions of the consultants you're considering working with, make sure you talk to clients who have already worked with them. Try to get a sense from these other clients about whether the consultant's are in it just for the thrill or they are really interested in seeing their clients succeed.

Why would those criteria matter? Well, when you choose a consultant, you are agreeing to give that person the e-mail addresses of all your employees so that he or she can send phishing e-mails to your staff. Some of those e-mails may ask for credentials or contain personal details, so you want to be able to trust that any consultant you hire will handle these situations properly.

Summary

It is estimated that 145 billion e-mails are sent every hour. I have read some reports that state 50 percent of all e-mail is malicious, others say 30 percent, others say 20 percent. Let's just say that if 20 percent is malicious, we can estimate that in the last hour 29 billion malicious e-mails hit inboxes around the globe. Twenty-nine billion, which is 29,000,000,000! Staggering.

This problem is not going away, but you can fight back. You can help your company defend itself and mitigate phishing attacks. As we've tried to explain in this book, there is no magic pill or one-stop solution to make this happen, but with hard work, persistence, and good planning you can succeed.

By now you know that Michele and I feel that phishing is a major problem that everyone must focus on, but we realize that this is not the only issue you have to fix. I know, all too well, that you also have to worry about all aspects of security awareness—networking, human, and everything in between.

Michele and I hope that this book will help you with your job. And if you are reading this but are not in a corporate IT department, then I hope this helps you understand why phishing education is vital to staying secure both at work and at home.

Stay a critical thinker, don't trust those links, slow down, and inspect a little more closely. If you do these things, you can give yourself a much better chance of not getting caught in the hooks of a phisher.

Stay secure.

Notes

1. Anti-Phishing Working Group, "Phishing Activity Trends Report, 2nd Quarter 2014," August 29, 2014, http://docs.apwg.org/reports/apwg_trends_report_q2_2014.pdf.

2. Google, Inc. and the University of California, San Diego, "Handcrafted Fraud and Extortion: Manual Account Hijacking in the Wild," retrieved November 11, 2014, http://services.google.com/fh/files/blogs/google_hijacking_study_2014.pdf.

3. EMC, "2013 a Year in Review," January 2014, http://www.emc.com/collateral/fraud-report/rsa-online-fraud-report-012014.pdf.

Index